The *Complete* SCHIPPERKE

An original painting by Heinrich Brendel of a Flemish Horse Fair with a Schipperke, painted on panel, circa 1855, of French or Dutch origin. The artist lived from 1827 to 1878 and was noted for domestic scenes and horses. *(From the collection of Lynn Brown)*

The *Complete*
SCHIPPERKE

The
SCHIPPERKE CLUB
of America

HOWELL
BOOK HOUSE

New York
Maxwell Macmillan Canada
Toronto
Maxwell Macmillan International
New York   Oxford   Singapore   Sydney

Howell Book House
Macmillan Publishing Company
866 Third Avenue
New York, NY 10022

Maxwell Macmillan Canada, Inc.
1200 Eglinton Avenue East
Suite 200
Don Mills, Ontario M3C 3N1

Macmillan Publishing Company is part of the Maxwell Communication Group of Companies.

Library of Congress Cataloging-in-Publication Data

The Complete Schipperke / the Schipperke Club of America.
    p.   cm.
  ISBN 0-87605-303-7
  1. Schipperke. I. Schipperke Club of America.
SF429.S36C65 1993
636.7'2—dc20   92-18287
                                        CIP

Macmillan books are available at special discounts for bulk purchases for sales promotions, premiums, fund-raising, or educational use. For details, contact:

Special Sales Director
Macmillan Publishing Company
866 Third Avenue
New York, NY 10022

10 9 8 7 6 5 4 3 2 1

Printed in the United States of America

Dedicated to Schipperke fanciers throughout the world, whose love for the "little black devils" has made the Schipperke what it is today.

Contents

Acknowledgments

When I was first appointed coordinator of *The Complete Schipperke* by the Board of Directors of the Schipperke Club of America, Inc., I was overwhelmed with the enormity of the task. Then, as I began to review past letters, books, articles, and notes, I realized that many others had made the task easier.

In a very real sense, F. Isabel Ormiston, Vella Root, Janice Martin, Mr. F. E. Verbanck of Ghent, Belgium, Roy Henre, Walter Chute, and Harold Claussen contributed much to this book.

Sincere thanks go to William and Marcia Bailey (Dream On Kennels), Wilma Dame (Wil-Cle Kennels), Kathy Gaul-Montgomery (Kleingaul Kennels), Tom and Carol Luke (Chatelet Kennels) for the invaluable help and materials they provided in the way of historical documents, pedigrees, photographs, bitch and stud dog statistics in addition to their advice, encouragement, and support.

Thanks also go to Melanie Howell and Terry Laney who helped type the material, George Photo Shop in Thousand Oaks, and all Schipperke fanciers and breeders who so generously sent information to me on their dogs, kennels, and history.

I particularly want to thank Lee Gumprecht for his moral support, encouragement, willingness to lend a hand whenever necessary, and above all, his sense of humor.

Without all of these wonderful people, this book could never be.

KATHLEEN BAKER-GUMPRECHT

The
Complete
SCHIPPERKE

An old lithograph of England's Queen Alexandria, her grandchildren, and dogs by artist Fre.
(From the collection of Lynn Brown)

1

The Origin of
the Schipperke

THE EXACT ORIGIN of the Schipperke was never actually documented and therefore is buried in the shadows of history. However, early Belgian authorities believe the breed originated principally in Flanders and the provinces of Antwerp and Brabant.

IN LEGEND

In the fifteenth century a monk named Wenceslas recorded an unusual story in his journals. According to Wenceslas, two shoemakers quarreled because a small dog belonging to the first shoemaker was making unwanted forays onto the property of the second.

Angry about the dog's trespasses, the second shoemaker showed his anger by cutting the tail entirely off his neighbor's dog. Other shoemakers decided that the little animal was better looking without the rear appendage, thus creating the custom of the tailless Schipperke. This account, claimed to be the earliest written mention of the breed, establishes that the trade guilds of Brussels possessed a house dog without a tail; surely no other but the Schipperke!

The Schipperke figures prominently in a sixteenth century English legend concerning William of Orange. This William was not William III of England, but the earlier and much greater Stadtholder, William the Silent, ''le Taisuex,''

1533–1584. William is still regarded as a national hero in both Holland and Belgium because, for a time, he united the seventeen provinces which comprised the two countries. The great National Belgian novel, De Coster's "Tyl Ulenspiegal," details his conquests.

William was determined to sever the Spanish hold upon the Netherlands, thus earning the eternal enmity of the Spanish King. After repeated attempts to capture William ended in failure, the superstitious Spaniards proclaimed that William was either the Devil himself or had a Devil as his familiar, as he was able to vanish rapidly and completely when pursued. The actual truth was more simple—the common people hid their hero.

A circumstance which struck fear into the hearts of William's enemies and lent credence to their superstitious fears was the medieval belief that when the Devil took the form of an animal, that animal was never complete. It was also strongly believed that a favorite disguise of Satan was the form of a black dog. Legends from all parts of Europe during the middle ages mark the appearance of the Devil in this disguise time and again. Therefore, imagine the horror of the people of Spain when they saw William followed by a black dog without a tail!

A pair of Schipperkes are credited with saving William's life during an assassination attempt. The would-be murderer lay in wait, and eventually crept up behind William. But before he could strike the fatal blow, a whirling mass of jet black animals, screaming curses and breathing fire, sprang upon him. The crowning horror was that the beasts were tailless! He confessed this when captured after he fled in terror, leaving William unharmed. William the Silent was murdered in 1584, apparently when the faithful little dogs were not at his side.

Another mention of the Schipperke occurs in the diary of Samuel Pepys, 1663–1703, Secretary to the Admiralty in England. Mr. Pepys traveled to France, where he met and married a French woman. After their marriage, Mrs. Pepys moved to England with her new husband, bringing a black Schipperke bitch from French Flanders with her. Mr. Pepys named the little dog Bete Noire, and grew to love the little dog wholeheartedly. However, Mrs. Pepys also loved the dog fiercely, and eventually Mr. Pepy's diary chronicled repeated quarrels between the couple over the Schipperke.

IN FACT

The known history of the breed begins in 1690 when the shoemakers in the St. Gery quarter organized a competitive exhibition of Schipperkes on designated Sundays on the Grand' Place in Brussels. The workmen exercised their ingenuity by making collars of hammered or carved brass for their Schipperkes. Always kept gleaming, these collars were worn only on Sundays and were fastened in a manner designed to pull out as few hairs as possible from the ruff.

One hundred and fifty years later (1830–1840), the Schipperke remained very fashionable in Brussels and, curiously enough, was protected by the disciples

2

of Saint Crispin. Even in this later period, it was still the custom to adorn Schipperkes with enormous collars of worked brass which were often real works of art. On Sundays one could see a shoemaker going out with or without his wife or children but never without his Schipperke. Although he could readily forget to shine his boots, he would never forget to polish the dog's collar.

During this period of early development, the breed was known by two names, giving rise to controversies on the true origin of the breed. The people of Brussels used the colloquial name "Spitz" or "Spitzke" to describe the small black dog. This name sheds little light on the breed's ancestry because several breeds which are referred to as a "Spitz" in Germany or America are called "Loulou" in Belgium. Thus, no relationship to these breeds is established by the Belgian call name.

Mr. F. Verbanck of Ghent, a noted Belgian authority of the breed, summed up his thoughts on this subject very well when he wrote: "If the spitz group is composed of *all* the nordic dogs, the German Shepherd and the other continental sheepdogs of the wolf-type as well as the Collie and the Shetland Sheepdog, then the Schipperke is also a spitz. But, if the spitz is *limited* to the group of German Wolfspitz breeds which now includes the Keeshond of Holland, then the Schipperke is not a spitz."

Over the years, various writers outside Belgium have claimed a Spitz origin for the Schipperke. One well-known dog chart even shows the Schipperke as a direct descendant of the Pomeranian. Victor Fally, a founder of the Belgium Schipperkes Club, debated the possibility of such an origin, writing: "It is true that the Pomeranian and the Schipperke resemble each other just as they resemble the sheepdogs. They belong to the same original stem which corresponds to a primitive type spread throughout the regions of the North and Baltic Seas which is related to the Norwegian, Swedish and even the Eskimo breeds. [But] it is impossible for the Pomeranian, itself, to have served to create the Schipperke because the latter has been revealed to have existed here before the introduction of the Pomeranian. The Schipperke has an entirely different aspect."

Another interesting point of comparison, which may also shed some light on tracing the ancestry of the Schipperke, is its natural tail carriage. Although most twentieth century literature maintains that the undocked tail of a Schip is carried over the back like a Spitz, early authorities are in disagreement with this assertion. Some years ago, the eminent Belgian judge, Charles Huge, and Victor Fally wrote that those Schipperkes left with a tail carry it like a Groenendael Sheepdog or Shepherd. For proof, in an earlier French dog book by M. Megnin, there is a photograph of a Schipperke with a tail carried straight like that of a sporting dog. Mr. Fally also contended that an undocked Schipperke with its tail curled over the back like a Pug or a Spitz is evidence that there has been crossbreeding in its ancestry, regardless of the names appearing in the pedigree.

Some English authorities have stated that the undocked tails of the Schipperke are carried in two ways; some are straight like a shepherd and others are carried curved over the back. It is believed likely that there has been occasional crossbreeding to some Spitz breed, particularly the Pomeranian, but the possible Spitz-like characteristics resulting from such crossbreeding is not considered evidence of the original derivation of the Schipperke.

The renowned French phylogeneticist, Dr. Herout, concluded that the Schipperke descended along the same morphological lines of the Spitz group. He based this belief on a theory postulated by Pierre Megnin. Simply described, canine specimens are broken down into four fundamental groups, taking into consideration their cephalic conformation and their general conformation. They are:

1. *Lupines*: the oldest branch in Dogdom. They have a resemblance to the wolf, which may be why many people believe that the dog descended from the wolf. Lupines have a cuneiform (cuneal) head, weak stop, and straight ears. The specimens most commonly portrayed are the Shepherd (German Shepherd Dog, Belgian Shepherd, etc.) and the Spitz breeds.
2. *Mollossoides* (Mastiffs): they have a rounded head with a voluminous skull, a short heavy muzzle, well-defined stop, and drooping ears. These include St. Bernards, Bullmastiffs, etc.
3. *Graioides*: characterized by a narrow and long head without stop and a pointed muzzle. All the Greyhounds are included in this category.
4. *Bracoides*: they have a medium-long head with a stop well defined, a rather large and generally long muzzle about the same length as the skull, and drooping ears. Occidental hunting dogs such as Beagles, Harriers, etc., are in this group.

These classifications correspond to the appearance of their particular breeds. Many breeds which do not conform to any of the four classifications could be the result of numerous crossbreedings among many breeds, either by chance or by human intervention. Among the descendants of these crossbreedings, the Lupo-Mollossoides, the Braco-Graioides, the Braio-Braco-Mollossoides can be identified. However, there are certain breeds where it is difficult, indeed even impossible, to recognize the categories from which they originated.

Dr. Herout believed there was no doubt as to the Schipperke's origin, contending the breed was one of the purest representatives of the Lupines. This, he argued, was why the breed remained unchanged in general appearance for a long period of time.

The name Schipperke was apparently introduced and used by boat captains who piloted their vessels between Brussels and Antwerp. According to these Antwerp boat men, the word Schipperke came from the Flemish word for boat, "schip," and meant "little boat man," or, as more commonly known in America, "little captain." It was partly because of possible confusion with the German Spitz breeds that the breed was officially renamed Schipperke. Despite the official recognition of the name, the breed is still commonly called Spitz by the layman in Belgium.

It has been suggested that the boat captains were responsible for the elimination of the Schipperke tail, as a dog minus this appendage was less likely to upset goods upon the narrow boat decks. However, there is no proof that the captains created the breed nor even possessed the largest number of them. This allegation was partially substantiated in the early twentieth century by Joseph Verbanck, a brother to Florimond Verbanck, an avid Schipperke fancier. Prior to 1930, Joseph Verbanck operated a barge line on the Ruhr between Rotterdam and Paris and procured several Schipperkes as watchdogs for his boats. He later wrote: "Let me say that these purebred Schipperkes created surprise and envy among the other shippers, but, when they heard about the prices paid for them, their interest abated immediately and they returned to their crossbreeds at giveaway prices. This will confirm that Schipperkes have never been used regularly as watchdogs on barges."

The little black dogs were found more widely distributed throughout various towns of central Belgium in the homes of middle class business people and among the members of the trade guilds. These people thought of the Schipperke as a diminutive shepherd and believed that the word Schipperke was derived through a corruption of the word for shepherd, "scheper," and thus meant "little shepherd." Impressed with the resemblance in appearance and characteristics between the Schipperke and the native sheepdog of Belgium (not to be confused with the Belgian Sheepdog known in the show ring today), these fanciers concluded that the Schipperke is the diminutive of the latter. Many arguments support this theory.

For one, there existed an intermediate type of dog, now extinct, which possessed many of the characteristics and the same general appearance of these two breeds. This dog, called the "Leuvenaar," was frequently seen in the region of Louvain accompanying wagoners and messengers traveling the route between Brussels and Louvain. Also tailless, this dog is described by early authorities as an all black, small-sized dog with a lively and active nature and weighing between 10 to 12 kilograms (22 and 26½ pounds). This indigenous sheepdog was very common in the County of Flanders and the Duchy of Brabant during the sixteenth and seventeenth centuries. Some were still in existence at the turn of the present century, but they now appear to be extinct. It is believed that the workmen and business people living in the cities of those regions chose the smallest specimens for use as watchdogs and ratters, characteristics which are an integral part of our Schipperkes today. One of the early presidents of the Schipperkes Club, who was also a judge, particularly favored these dogs and insisted that this variety should never become lost. He was well known for preferring the largest exhibits when judging, even to the point of awarding first place to dogs whose weight exceeded the maximum limit of the Standard.

A further argument for the relationship between the Schipperke and these sheepdogs is in the natural herding ability exhibited by some of the larger Schipperkes when given the proper opportunity to exercise it. Thus, the Leuvenaar was considered as the missing link uniting the Schipperke to the sheepdog.

After due consideration, the Belgium Schipperkes Club founders accepted, as the most logical explanation, the belief that the Schipperke is in reality a diminutive shepherd and that he was derived from the small native black Belgian sheepdog. Belgian canine authorities consistently supported this origin down through the years. Before learning of the Belgian theory, Dr. Leon Whitney, renowned veterinarian and author, placed the Schipperke as a sheepdog. Felix Lese, past vice-president of the Eskimo Sled Dog Club of America, wrote F. Isabel Ormiston the following statement: "Your claim that the Schipperke is a diminutive Belgian Sheepdog is to me an additional reason to believe that the Schipperke is a member of the Samoyed group, for there again many authorities place both the Alsatian (German Shepherd) and the Belgian Sheepdog in that classification also."

A further complication to tracing the breed's origin is the fact that many old dog books and magazine articles erroneously designate the Schipperke as a Dutch breed originating in Holland. This may be because the Flemish language is a form of Dutch. Hence, the word Flanders has been interpreted to mean Holland instead of the Flemish provinces of Belgium. In addition, Belgium and Holland were united against their common oppressor Spain for a time. They were again one for a few years after the Battle of Waterloo, but by 1815 long separation had aroused certain antagonisms. The countries separated for the final time in 1830. The elder Louis Vander Snickt, a founder of the Schipperkes Club and a noted discoverer of Belgian breeds, put the theory that the Schipperke was a Dutch breed to rest when he wrote in 1886: "the Schipperke is, perhaps, the only indisputable Belgian dog that we possess." It is the hope of fanciers today that the Schipperke breed may always thrive in Belgium, its native home.

2

The Nineteenth Century: The Development of the Breed in Belgium and England

BELGIUM

In THE EARLY nineteenth century, the Schipperke was widely found throughout central Belgium. It was practically the only house dog known there until 1880.

On July 21st, 1880, the year of the fiftieth anniversary of Belgian independence, a group of hunting-dog fanciers organized the second Belgian dog show (the first took place in 1847). Held in Brussels at the old army exercising plain, the show drew an entry of nearly a thousand dogs. One of the guiding spirits of this exposition, the Comte de Beauffort, sponsored a special class in honor of the national dog of Belgium. This class was designated as "short-coated terriers, all black, with erect ears, without a tail, a Flemish breed, Schipperkes." Although three prizes were offered, not one Schipperke was entered.

Apparently, the devotees of the breed were not aware their modest companion could be raised to the status of a show dog. Despite the failure to attract any Schipperkes, overall the show was a success and provided the impetus for the foundation of a canine society which was named for the patron saint of hunting. Thus, the Société Saint-Hubert was established in 1882 for the purpose of improving canine breeds in Belgium, with the Comte de Beauffort as its first president. By royal favor, this society was granted the title of Société Royale Saint-Hubert on Sept. 26, 1885.

One of the first projects of the new society was the creation of a stud book, *Livres des Origines St. Hubert*, or "L.O.S.H." modeled after the Stud Book of the Kennel Club of England, the first volume recorded canine events to the end of 1882 and was published in 1883. Since then, the L.O.S.H. has been published regularly except for the two periods of occupation during the World Wars.

From the beginning of the Société Royale St. Hubert, the Schipperke was considered a pure breed and allowed registration in the very first stud book, whereas a relative, the Belgian Sheepdog, was not granted registration privileges until some years later. In the first volume of the L.O.S.H., the Schipperke was cataloged as: "Short-coated terriers, with erect ears, tailless, a Flemish breed, Schipperkes." Each Schipperke was registered as "black" in the first few volumes but later books omitted the color, as the breed was considered as being black only.

The first inscriptions recorded sire and dam as "origin unknown." Official breeding was only begun in 1882 with the creation of the first stud book, and it would have been useless to name the sire and dam if the parents themselves were not registered. An exception is the registration record of the very first Schipperke, Tip (#146), for which the parents and breeder are given. This may be because Tip's owner, a fancier of English shooting dogs, was acquainted with systematic breeding practices.

Not until the fifth volume of the L.O.S.H. did there appear an inscription of a Schipperke having both parents of registered origin. Two such Schipperkes are listed, but their origin is limited to one generation only. It was not until several years later that pedigrees of the majority of the registered dogs could be extended further than the grandparents. As a result, it has to be accepted as an axiom that, regardless of their appearance as purebred Schipperkes, some Schipperke foundation stock, could have some ancestor deviating from the true type in their genetic make-up. Therefore, a throwback could occur from time to time. Hence, in the words of a Belgian authority, "it is the duty of the conscientious breeder to eliminate such throwbacks and never try to claim them as representative of the true breed."

Prior to registration, the Schipperke had been bred in Belgium by following certain oral canons but without any fixed written Standard and without any kind of registering. Breeders relied solely on their memory in keeping the breed pure. These first registrations illustrate a panorama in the growth process toward the birth of a pure strain selected from a breed indigenous to Belgium and present there for many, many years.

The first Schipperkes to be exhibited appeared at the Spa Dog Show in 1882. First prize went to Tip (by Spitz out of Finette), owned by Vicomte de Jonghe of Brussels and bred by M. J. Renier. Second prize went to Fintje (#147), owned by Baron J. Van Havre of Antwerp. Also shown were Tic and Tac belonging to Madame Bodinus of Brussels. The following year at Ostende, six Schipperkes were shown; two were exhibited in Antwerp in 1884. In Brussels, nine were shown in 1885, thirteen in 1886, eleven in 1887, and thirteen again in 1888. During these first years the breed was judged without any formal requirements of an official standard.

It was at the Brussels show in 1885 that Queen Marie Henriette of Belgium was attracted by the little black dogs and expressed a desire to possess the winning dog, Blak (#942), exhibited by Mr. J. Coosemans. The acquisition of this dog by Her Majesty the Queen caused the Schipperke to become fashionable. The Queen was often seen accompanied by this dog. In 1888, the Countess of Flanders acquired Pitch (#1594) and further increased the prestige of the breed in Belgium.

DECLINE AND REBIRTH

During the years following 1880, in an interesting way, the breed gradually diminished in number until it nearly became extinct. Various Englishmen visiting Belgium were attracted by the Schipperke and took home a specimen. These little dogs, with their distinguished silhouette and endearing ways as devoted companions, so pleased the English that they became much in demand. Purchases were made in Belgium at ridiculous prices and exports to England multiplied until the Schipperke was threatened with extinction in its country of origin by 1890.

The Belgian people attached no great importance to the little dogs so common in their homes and on their streets. Because no group of fanciers was yet united in maintaining the breed as purebred, few people in Belgium realized that the process of increasing exports was detrimental to the welfare of the breed in its homeland. Further complicating matters was the fact that at the same time, the Belgian public acquired a preference for Fox Terriers, Pugs, Brussels Griffons, and following World War I, the Pekingese.

Realizing this situation was detrimental, in the latter part of the 1880s several Schipperke fanciers met to perpetuate the breed and prevent the degeneration in type. The slow progress of the breed, as demonstrated by the low show entries, was attributed to the divergence of opinion among the judges. One of the principal purposes of this group was to make a list of the characteristic points which later became known as the Standard for the breed.

The group recognized that there existed three known varieties of Schipperkes, which varied with the locality in which they originated. These differences were described in an article by E. R. Spalding in *The American Book of the Dog* (G. O. Shields, editor), published in 1891. Mr. Spalding quoted a letter written by John Lysen of Antwerp (a recognized authority on English Setters and other English bird dogs), which described the Antwerp, Louvain, and Brussels types of Schipperke.

The Louvain type had a smooth, shiny coat with little ruff, and a longer head with tall, narrow ears, and was sometimes described as terrier-like in appearance. The Brussels type had a much shorter head with large eyes, broad forehead, and unusually large ears set far apart and low on the head. This type usually had a fair, hard-haired ruff and good coat. Unfortunately, all the dogs of this group were also considerably at the elbows, which, added to their square short head, seemed to indicate a Bulldog cross. The Antwerp type seemed to be a combination of the other two and was the most attractive and most popular. This was a thickset dog having a distinct ruff and culotte of long hairs with shorter hairs on the sides of the body and on the legs. These dogs were also characterized by a long mane (jabot) extending down between the forelegs back to about half the body.

On January 29, 1888, the magazine, *Chasse Et Pêche*, published a proposed draft of the characteristic points for the breed. This Belgian sporting magazine was used as the official organ of the Schipperkes Club for a time and had much to do with the original success of the breed when the club was founded. A number of excellent articles about the Schipperke written by breed authorities were printed in this journal. More than fifty years later, publication was suspended because of hard times. Although resumed for a time, it is now no longer published.

Louis Vander Snickt invited fanciers and their dogs to meet on February 12, 1888, in a building on the Grand' Place in Brussels. Other persons who could

A flyer for Chenil de L'Esperance Kennels in Brussels, owned by Louis Vander Snickt. Mr. Vander Snickt was instrumental in organizing the first Schipperkes Club in Belgium in 1888. The dog pictured is most likely his greatest winner, Ch. Toto de l'Esperance.

10

give information on Schipperkes were also invited. A second meeting took place seven days later. On March 4, 1888, the Schipperkes Club (Belgium) was founded and a provisional committee was nominated. Club members were composed of F. E. de Middeleer—president, Felix Van Buggenhoudt—secretary, Arthur Maes—treasurer, the Comte de Beauffort, and the Messrs. Gantois, Dardenne, John Proctor, Francois Reusens, Louis Vander Snickt, Victor Du Pre, Victor Fally, G. Massin, and J. Drossart. On March 11, 1888, the bylaws were adopted and on March 19 the points of the breed were established. The official standard, based upon the Antwerp variety of Schipperke, was adopted June 19, 1888, at a general assembly of the club members.

The members of the Schipperkes Club met again on June 24, 1888. They had obtained the patronage of the Société Royale St. Hubert in May and decided to hold a Specialty Show in Brussels on August 11 and 12, 1888. Classes for the Brussels Griffon were to be provided and there were even classes for brass collars for Schipperkes. The Schipperkes Club voted on and became the first club to allow dogs to compete in different classes by paying an entry fee for each class. The show was a great success, drawing seventy-seven Schipperkes in eleven classes as well as thirty-four Brussels Griffons and eight Schipperke collars. The formation of the Schipperkes Club increased the breed's popularity greatly in Belgium in succeeding years.

The success of the club's first specialty show is a measure of the excellent results obtained by this group in its initial efforts. Among those fanciers forming the Schipperkes Club was Mr. Reusens, an ardent Schipperke breeder, who kept specimens of the breed on the canal boats he operated between Brussels and Antwerp. Mr. Reusens has been called "The Father of the Schipperke" in Belgium because of his enthusiasm for and promotion of the breed and because he established the first regular kennel under the prefix "Exter."

In 1888, Mr. Reusens recorded Spitz B (#1605), whelped in 1885 as his first L.O.S.H. registered Schipperke, and later owned a remarkable specimen called Franz (#3055). Like most Schipperkes of his time, Franz was registered "unknown origin." He served as a foundation stud from which the present day Schipperke has evolved. This dog so pleased the fanciers of his day that Franz was chosen as representing the ideal type of the breed. A popular belief in Belgium was that Franz served as the model for writing the original Belgian Standard. This is incorrect, however. Registration records confirm that Franz was whelped in December 1889, more that one year after the Standard was officially adopted.

Although no photograph of Franz exists, he does appear in a painting by A. Clarys which has been reproduced in several books. For those who saw Franz, the Standard was considered a sufficiently precise description of him and gives an idea of his exact appearance. Franz's back was short and his topline sloped downward slightly from the neck. The only criticism recorded of him was that his muzzle was a "trifle short and appeared squared off at the end due to the lower jaw being a shade too long in relation to the upper jaw." His teeth met

A painting of Exter Albert (#4196) by noted artist A. Clarys. Albert was bred by F. Ruesens, who owned a barge line between Brussels and Antwerp. Born March 26, 1895, Albert's sire was the eminent Franz (#3055) and his dam was Joelleke (#3497).

evenly and he was not undershot. Franz's head was expressive—short ears, well cut and close together when erect; small eyes, oval in shape, and a frank and questioning expression—as if he were always asking his disciples, "What is it?"

Additional information concerning the early years of the Belgium Schipperkes Club was recorded in the Annual Reports of the Secretary of the Société Royale St. Hubert. These records reflect that the Schipperkes Club was the first breed club officially organized in Belgium, followed shortly after by the Club du Griffon Bruxellois in 1889. The two clubs then joined together until 1904.

The Secretary wrote that these two clubs held "a brilliant show under the patronage of the Société St. Hubert in August 1889. Two hundred and twenty-two dogs were assembled at Parc Leopold in Brussels. . . . This interesting show attracted a great number of visitors, including several members of the royal family." In a 1907 volume of the L.O.S.H., the Secretarial report stated, "The Club du Griffon Bruxellois and the Schipperkes Club, united together until 1904, have been the means of developing a fondness for these two interesting breeds.

A lithograph of "Brave Spitz" by artist A. Clarys which appeared in the dog magazine *Chasse et Pêche*. Brave Spitz was owned by Heer A. Vanbuggenhoudt of Brussels, Belgium.

The shows they have organized together during this period have demonstrated this in a splendid manner.''

During the period covered by the first twenty-five volumes of the L.O.S.H. (1882–1907) some of the breeders who became well known in the breed and whose names were frequently repeated in the registration inscriptions were: C. F. Crousse, E. Rombouts, F. E. de Middeleer, Van Buggenhoudt, F. Reusens, Fl. Duchateau, and J. Drossart.

ENGLAND

The first traceable recorded importation of Schipperkes into England was by J. M. Berrie in 1887, when he acquired a bitch in whelp named Flo. Soon afterward, between 1887 and 1890, Mr. A. George, Mr. G. Krehl, and Mr. E. Joachim imported the males Drieske, Shtoots, and Fritz of Spa from Belgium. These dogs became first Schipperke champions in England and were also the foundation stock for the breed there.

The Schipperke Club (England) was founded in 1890, determined to advance and promote the Schipperke in England. A duly elected committee recommended that the Belgian Standard be adopted as the breed Standard in England. This was approved with one exception—the weight of the "ideal schipperke" was changed from 10 pounds to 12 pounds, thereby removing the Schipperke from possible classification into the Toy Group.

In February of 1890, Mr. Joachim was involved in a scandal over a bitch named Aunt Chloe. At a show where he was judging Schipperkes, he took a strong liking to Aunt Chloe and purchased her from the exhibitor, E. Durrant. Mr. Durrant had only owned the bitch for two weeks, having purchased her from a south coast resort in January 1890. Soon after Mr. Joachim acquired Aunt Chloe, he discovered that Chloe had a large patch of white fur on her chest which had been dyed black. He reported the deception to the English Kennel Club and the matter was investigated. Ultimately, the Kennel Club took no action against Mr. Durrant because there was no proof that he had been aware of the dyed fur and he had purchased the dog in good faith.

While most early English Schipperkes were solid black, there were other colors reported, including fawn, sable, and blue. Mr. Durrant eventually became quite taken with non-black Schipperkes and attempted to breed them. He met with limited success because his colored stock produced predominantly black puppies.

The year 1894 was one of turmoil. In October, a letter was circulated to Schipperke fanciers by A. Frehl (a founding member of The Schipperke Club) advising the membership that he had resigned as the club president and as a member because of a disagreement with the vice president. Mr. Frehl he argued that the type of Schipperke winning in England was contrary to the Belgian type. He described the Schipperkes he had seen in Belgium and compared them to the English type.

He purchased Belgian Ch. Hubert from Mr. Reusens to demonstrate to English fanciers that the English dogs were "black, prick-eared, wire-haired terriers, *alias* Schipperkes" and "not the true type." Mr. Frehl then founded the "St. Hubert Schipperke Club" and offered Ch. Hubert at stud to any St. Hubert club member with a three guinea stud fee. Eventually the furor of this controversy faded and fanciers continued to show and breed Schipperkes throughout the remainder of the century.

3

The Schipperke in the United States

THE HONOR of importing the first Schipperke to the United States is disputed but seems to belong to Mr. Walter Comstock of Providence, Rhode Island. He imported a pair of Schipperkes in 1889. These dogs, named Midnight and Darkness, came directly to Boston from Antwerp on a freight boat. They are most likely the two Schipperkes pictured in the illustration for an article by Spalding in the book, *The American Book of the Dog* (1891).

THE EARLY DAYS

There is a possibility, however, that the breed may have existed in America, temporarily, at a much earlier time. In an old book, F. Isabel Ormiston found a picture illustrating General Charles Lee of Revolutionary War fame. General Lee was captured by the British at Basking Ridge, New Jersey, and this illustration depicts him accompanied by a dog showing decided Schipperke characteristics, except that it had a tail. The dog was not a Pomeranian for it had a short coat, marked ruff and culotte, and a rather longer and sharper head. At this juncture of American history, portions of New Jersey had been settled by many Dutch and Belgian immigrants. Although there is no conclusive proof, it is known that Schipperkes were well established in Belgium long before pre-Revolutionary War days, and a logical possibility exists that some of these settlers brought their faithful Schipperkes with them when they migrated to America.

America also felt some reaction to the English craze for Schipperkes of the

Celtic des Bois Mures won a Best in Show award when only a year old at the Specialty show in Brussels in 1928 over the favorite, Ch. Arsouille de l'Erebe. She was exported to France by Dr. Alexis before she had secured her Belgian title, but won her French championship in short order. She was later purchased by Kelso Kennels and won her American championship as well.

late 1880s. The American craze, however, was short lived. So great was the demand for anything called a Schipperke that nearly every ship from Belgium carried the product of the "Antwerp Sunday market," or, in fact, anything to which the name of Schipperke could be given.

Worse, in America itself, small black mutts were crossed with the Spitz to produce something that might be termed a Schipperke. The result was that admirers became discouraged and very soon the demand died down, although some fanciers kept breeding. A book printed in 1893 carried an advertisement for Schipperkes by Mr. Frederick W. Connolly and contained a picture of "Cople Sophia."

During the late 1800s, the Comstock dogs were shown a few times, but Mr. Comstock was unsuccessful in breeding them. As a matter of fact, Mr. Comstock once wrote that the bitch was a persistent runaway, and after chasing her all over the state, he finally gave her away.

1900 TO 1930

Although Schipperkes appeared in America in the previous century, the first representative of the breed was not registered in the American Kennel Club

Stud Books until 1904. During this same decade, Frank Dole imported several Schipperkes and showed them extensively in the Miscellaneous classes. His efforts were rewarded—the American Kennel Club officially recognized the Schipperke breed and a number of people adopted them. A breed club (also a member of the American Kennel Club) was formed. This club's first president was Colonel Denny, who later became a leading Schipperke authority in the United States prior to World War I.

Colonel Denny bred Ch. Tar and Ch. Flyette, who were owned by Mrs. Schriber of New York. Mr. George Ronsse was active in the breed by 1905 and was called the leading spirit of the first American Schipperke club. An old edition of the Encyclopedia Britannica was illustrated with an unidentified Schipperke owned by Mr. Ronsse. He also owned Togo R, a direct descendant of the famed Belgian dog, Franz. Togo R's picture was used to illustrate the breed in *The Dog Book* by James Watson printed in 1906. Another fancier, Mr. Willard Aborn, Wicklow Kennels, bred more than 100 Schipperkes in the early period before World War I. He owned Ch. Wicklow Rastus and Ch. Wicklow Constance.

Frank Dole showed Teddy R to championship in 1910. Although Ch. Teddy R was imported from England, his pedigree indicated that he was from Belgian-bred parents. Although erroneously described as the first Schipperke imported to America, he arrived more than ten years after the Comstock pair. However, this dog does seem to have been the first Schipperke to make a permanent impression on the breed in this country.

A list of the Best of Breed awards made at the Westminster Kennel Club shows from 1910 to 1927 includes the number of Schipperkes entered each year. In 1910, eighteen Schipperkes were shown. Thereafter 29, 27, 30, 23, and 29 Schipperkes were entered and shown, the last large entry occurring in the year 1915.

The first World War affected the number of entries. In 1916, only eight Schipperkes were shown at Westminster, followed by an entry of fifteen in 1917. Thereafter, entries remained very low until the late 1920s. Best of Breed at Westminster was awarded only once during this period, in 1918, to Happy Boy (AKC #247376). After World War I, Westminster no longer represented the largest entry in Schipperkes during the year.

The first breed club flourished until World War I but left no permanent imprint on the breed. One member, Mr. Aborn, claimed that the club was a victim of the war, but another thought the death of George Ronsse was the real cause of the break up. The Schipperkes owned by the members of this early club were equally of English and Belgian blood. These dogs did not appear to be of high quality according to pictures that survived into later times. The result of breeding these poorer specimens did not produce the best type of either country in the United States, causing the old American stock to run down and lose many of the attributes of the true Schipperke.

After World War I and into the early 1920s, the breed was at a low ebb. In the East, the Yperland Kennels had a few dogs and appeared at Westminster when only a few were being shown. This kept the public informed that there was such a breed as the Schipperke although there wasn't enough competition in those days to complete the requirements for a championship. A good little dog and the 1928 Westminster winner, Thistlewood Falcon, campaigned for years but was not able to meet enough competition to make his title.

Another fancier during these lean years was Mr. R. Culbertson of Chicago, who bred and exhibited in the early 1920s. Mr. Culbertson preferred larger Schipperkes, and anything under sixteen pounds seemed a Toy to him. One of his breeding, Broadcast, was the favorite of Irene Castle McLaughlin for a number of years. Later, Mr. Culbertson moved to Minnesota, keeping only a few dogs. Most of his stock went to the West Coast.

Along the Pacific Coast show entries increased somewhat in the 1920s and Ch. Samarand, his litter sister Ch. Demi Tasse, and Ch. Kim, bred by Mrs. E. C. Rand of Santa Rosa, California, all became champions. Mrs. Rand also bred Ch. Wallyrand, a dog owned by Grace Wallace, who was reported to have been undefeated in the breed. Many other dogs bred by Mrs. Rand made championship and in turn produced champions.

The Ormiston Influence—Kelso Kennels

It was during this period in the early 1920's that Miss F. Isabel Ormiston became interested in Schipperkes. Dissatisfied with the quality of the American stock for starting her Schipperke kennel, she traveled to England, France, and Belgium in search of the best possible dogs. While in Europe, she researched the breed, its origin and history, then selected her foundation stock, choosing only those Belgian bred dogs which were winners in good competition in their native land. For her first Schipperke she selected a bitch, Flore de Veeweyde, and imported her to the United States in 1924. The next year she returned to Belgium and chose her foundation stud, Max de Veeweyde, becoming the first of numerous champions. Not only did "Max" and "Flore" found the renowned Kelso Schipperke Kennels, but they also furnished the bloodlines which formed the foundation of many other Schipperke Kennels in the United States. Nearly all Schipperkes making championship today can trace their ancestry back to Max and Flore in some way, and many are multiple descendants of these two.

Miss Ormiston continued to import the best Schipperkes obtainable in Belgium until World War II. Many of these dogs were Belgian or French champions of outstanding quality, and several were bitches bred to the best Belgian sires. For the first three years, while competition in the East was meager, Kelso Kennels did very little exhibiting. Instead, Miss Ormiston spent time breeding stock to build up her kennel. She also wrote articles about Schipperkes to publicize the Belgian type and to disseminate correct information on the breed's history in its native land.

To fully understand the enormity of this task, one must be aware that the original American stock resembled the old Louvain type of Schipperke which

Two views of the famed Kelso Kennels at 134 Lake Road in Bernardsville, New Jersey. The kennels can be clearly seen in the lower picture.

had become obsolete in Belgium. There was little data on the breed origin and early history available in the United States, and various erroneous statements were circulated in those days (some of which even persist to this day!). In addition, many Schipperkes of this era had been imported to this country from England, their main characteristic being the shorter coat minus the longer, fuller ruff and culotte demanded by the Belgians.

Having studied Schipperkes in their native land, including research at the

IDEAL HEAD CH. FLORE de VEEWEYDE, IMP.
KELSO KENNELS, BERNARDSVILLE, N.J.

A head study of Ch. Flore de Veeweyde and F. Isabel Ormiston's handwritten notation that she possessed an "ideal head." Miss Ormiston imported Flore to the United States from Belgium in 1924. She was the foundation bitch of Kelso Kennels.

University of Ghent, Miss Ormiston expended much energy to bring correct information to the American public. Her efforts aroused the animosity of several breeders who had English and older American stock, including George A. Cranfield of Santa Monica, California. Probably the most active and extensive Schipperke breeder on the West Coast during the postwar era of the 1920s and 1930s, Mr. Cranfield was not only a breeder and exhibitor but also an importer, judge, and very prolific writer on the breed. As a confirmed devotee of the English

Champion Max de Veeweyde the foundation stud dog of the famed Kelso Kennels. Max was imported to the United States by F. Isabel Ormiston in 1925 and sired many Kelso champions.   *Tauskey*

Schipperke, he was a strong antagonist of Miss Ormiston's and publicly opposed her efforts to establish the Belgian Standard in the United States. He went so far as to offer free stud service to bitches of English breeding. Through his breed column in a dog magazine of that day, Mr. Cranfield led the opposition to the adoption of the Belgian Standard in this country. Perhaps the most important import he owned was My Billy Boy, who founded a bloodline still producing champions today through Ch. Coltness Little Skipper. Skipper formed the foundation for several of the successful Midwest kennels of the 1930s. Another English import, Royd Robbie, completed American championship and was the founder of another, but less prolific, male line which is still in existence. One of Mr. Canfield's imported bitches, Bette o'the North received much publicity but left little permanent impression on the breed today.

The controversy over the English versus Belgian types was waged bitterly in several canine journals of the day and expanded into an argument over the adoption of all solid colors in an American Standard for the breed. Despite the bitter and vigorous opposition waged by the devotees of these English dogs, Miss Ormiston's efforts in behalf of the Belgian type Schipperke resulted in the founding of The Schipperke Club of America, Inc., and its subsequent adoption of a breed standard which was essentially a direct translation of the Belgian one.

Ch. Dolette of Kelso with an unknown admirer on board an ocean liner from Europe. Dolette was the winner of two all-breed Best in Show awards in Belgium when she was imported to the United States by Kelso Kennels. Miss Ormiston once described Dolette as the ideal of her breed.

During the late 1920s, Kelso Kennels, owned jointly by F. Isabel Ormiston and her sister, Clara C. Ormiston, started showing extensively in the East and soon rose to the top in show wins. Over the next ten years, Kelso Kennels continued to import a number of Schipperkes from Belgium, several of which were class or championship certificate winners in that country. Among the most important of these which have founded champion-producing lines and families in this country are: Gallant of Kelso, Frida des Violettes of Kelso, Bebe de Ter Meeren of Kelso, Belg. Ch. Dolette de Veeweyde of Kelso, her daughter Fr. Ch. Celtic des Bois Mures, Nonette de Veeweyde of Kelso, and Garce de Veeweyde of Kelso. Bebe, Celtic, Nonette, and Garce all made American championships.

Kelso Kennels built up an unequaled record and reputation, having bred or owned more than 100 Schipperke champions. The word "Kelso" became synonymous with excellent quality. Many successful Schipperke kennels have since been founded with Kelso dogs or bloodlines. Indeed, most of the show

A challenge issued to F. Isabel Ormiston by George A. Cranfield of Santa Monica, California, which appeared in *Dog Topics* magazine in April of 1929. Mr. Cranfield was a proponent of the English type of Schipperke, Miss Ormiston favored the Belgium type. The challenge was never accepted.

winners in the United States today descend from the Kelso Schipperkes and their Belgian ancestors.

Standardizing the Breed

On October 15, 1927, a Schipperke received the first coveted Best in Show award in the United States. This honor was won by Yperland Jet Black Skipper (AKC #543212) at the Middlesex County Kennel Club show in Newton, Massachusetts. Skipper was bred by Yperland Kennels and owned by Dr. C. Hammett Rogers of Newport, Rhode Island. His sire was the Belgian import, Black de Veeweyde of Yperland, and his dam was an Yperland Peter Simon daughter. Curiously enough, this dog did not do well at other shows and was retired without attaining championship status.

As the serious exhibitors proceeded to compete regularly at dog shows, it began to be apparent that there was an urgent need for a breed club. Few shows provided classes for Schipperkes and fewer still offered any prizes. Judges were anyone who could do "and all other breeds," a classification including the Schipperke.

Much of the time, the breed was being judged by an English Standard. Without an official Standard, judging results were often inconsistent. In fact, one judge during this period was heard to inquire of the steward as to what a

F. Isabel Ormiston and her sister Clare pose with some Kelso champions of the 1930s.

Ch. Gallant of Kelso, a Belgian import. *Tauskey*

Schipperke looked like. Such a situation was not conducive to attracting sizeable entries nor to improving the breed. An active breed club became imperative. To this end, Mr. E. K. Aldrich, Jr., undertook the painstaking and laborious task of writing to every owner of a registered Schipperke in the United States to invite their help in founding a Schipperke club. One difficulty met in securing members was that a number of the breeders, with early American stock, opposed the adoption of a Belgian Standard, and some opposed the solid-black color requirement. Mr. Cranfield, the opposition leader, proclaimed that a few Schipperke breeders opposed the exclusion of color in the proposed Standard. The issue was decided when the American Kennel Club stated in writing that it would not accept a Standard allowing any color other than solid black.

THE SCHIPPERKE CLUB OF AMERICA

In April 1929, The Schipperke Club of America, Inc., was founded. At the first meeting, members adopted a Standard for the Schipperke which was essentially a direct translation of the Belgian Standard. The Club then applied for membership in the American Kennel Club and was accepted. As the American Kennel Club member club for the breed, The Schipperke Club of America, Inc., was accorded the designation of Parent Club, a position which granted it exclusive control over the breed Standard. It still holds this position today.

After the adopted Standard was approved by the Parent Club and the American Kennel Club, it became the official American Standard. Thereafter, the American Kennel Club denied registration to all non-black Schipperkes. Today, although colored Schipperkes can be registered and shown in Obedience, they are still disqualified in the conformation ring.

The efforts of the Club on behalf of the breed were rewarded by increased entries at shows and by the eventual establishment of the Belgian-type Schipperke in the United States. Judging improved gradually, but some confusion remained over interpretation of several points in the standard. Consequently, in 1935 the Schipperke Club of America, Inc., passed a revision which clarified the size requirement and emphasized the heavier coat with distinct ruff and culotte, the distinguishing characteristics of the Belgian Schipperke. From that time forward judging results gradually improved in quality.

One of the first projects of The Schipperke Club of America, Inc., was the publication of a club booklet to provide some information on the breed. A few years later, a revised booklet was printed to furnish more breed pictures for the education of the public. Still later, in 1940, an expanded book, which presented a more detailed history of the breed throughout the world, was published. This last book was revised in 1950. All these books were authored by F. Isabel Ormiston, founder member and club secretary, and printed from private donations. However, they were distributed through The Schipperke Club of America, Inc., as a service to the public for disseminating information on the breed. After

Ch. Rico of Kelso, owned by Clarence S. Howell of Connecticut.

Ch. 'Ti Noir of Kelso

26

the English breed book by Mr. E. B. Holmes, published in 1934, went out of print, these American books were the only ones on the Schipperke available anywhere at that time and distribution became international.

THE 1940s AND 1950s

In 1943 Mr. and Mrs. Carlton Jones acquired a Schipperke but did not begin showing until 1946. This outstanding dog, named Linarm, earned his championship title within a few weeks. This initial success spurred Mr. and Mrs. Jones to take up breeding and showing of Schipperkes and soon the May-He-Co name was being seen consistently at California shows. May-He-Co Kennels eventually owned or bred numerous champions. Then, in the 1950s, this kennel added outside bloodlines, which apparently introduced color-producing genes into their breeding stock. Mr. Jones then publicly stated his use of non-black Schipperkes for breeding, contending this was necessary for the continued progress of the breed. A few Schipperke breeders followed his example.

A vigorous confrontation ensued between Mr. Jones and Miss Ormiston and consequently, The Schipperke Club of America. Mr. Jones published a newsletter, forwarded free of charge to all Schipperke owners in the United States, in which he verbally berated Miss Ormiston and The Schipperke Club of America, Inc. Eventually, his membership privileges were suspended. Undaunted, he organized a nationwide breed club in opposition to The Schipperke Club of America, Inc. The American-Belgian Schipperke Club, Inc., was founded in 1951. Its intent appeared to be the promotion of the breeding of non-black Schipperkes. Although it functioned for several years, the American-Belgian Schipperke Club is no longer in existence. In 1959, The Schipperke Club of America, Inc., amended its Standard to state clearly the disqualification of any Schipperke of a color other than solid black.

From 1924 until her death in 1954, Miss Ormiston continued active in behalf of the Schipperke breed. She served continuously as Secretary of The Schipperke Club of America, Inc., from its inception, wrote numerous articles on the breed for various magazines and newspapers, conducted correspondence with Schipperke fanciers here and abroad, helped and advised sincere novices, translated many articles written by Belgian and French authorities, and wrote the breed column for the American Kennel Gazette. In addition, she wrote the only American books on the breed prior to the second World War.

Certainly, one of the greatest benefactors to the Schipperke in America was F. Isabel Ormiston. Her foundation work and influence will be felt for some time to come. To her, Schipperke fanciers are indebted for establishing the Belgian-type Schipperke in America and for leading in the development of the present-day American Schipperke, the short thickset dog with the longer coat of slightly harsh texture and the sloping backline.

Ch. Dina of Kelso, One of Ch. Maroufke of Kelso's thirty-two champion get.

4

Schipperke Fanciers in North America

THIS CHAPTER is to serve as a reference guide and includes many Schipperke fanciers in North America during the past ninety years. It is *not* an exhaustive list of every breeder or owner in the breed and is based on available resources. The names of fanciers and/or kennel names are arranged alphabetically. The era in the which the fancier was active appears after the kennel name. This is ONLY to pinpoint the decades the fancier was active, not to describe the length of time the kennel has been in existence. For example, a kennel started in 1979 and disbanded in 1983 will be listed as active in the "1970s/1980s." The name, state, and a description of their activities and Schipperkes follows.

A.R.E.S.—Active: early 1970s/present. Owners: Toni and Ellen Stevens of Missouri. Their best-known dogs include Ch. Do-Well's Nitro (Ch. Skipalong's Gadget ex Ch. Wilbet's Merry Mistletoe), an all-breed Best in Show winner. Nitro was awarded the Silver Certificate of Distinction by the "Kennel Review Top Producers" system as the sire of 25 champion offspring. More of his get have since finished their titles.

His get includes Ch. Padolin Missle Two of A.R.E.S. (ex Ch. Roetmop Aveline). During her show career (1974–1980) Missle was in direct competition with her sire and full brother, Ch. A.R.E.S. Beauregard O Padolin, yet still managed to collect 61 Best of Breed wins, 98 Best of Opposite Sex wins, 36 Group placements, 2 Specialty Best of Breeds awards and 8 Specialty Best of

29

Ch. Do-Well's Nitro earned many Best of Breed wins, Group placings, one Specialty win and an all-breed Best in Show. *Booth*

Opposite Sex awards. She was the Schipperke Club of America's Specialty Best of Opposite Sex winner and the SCA Top Winning Bitch in 1975, 1976, and 1977. Ch. A.R.E.S. Beauregard O Padolin finished his championship at seven months of age, winning three five-point majors in three shows held on February 4, 5, and 6, 1977. His overall wins include an all-breed Best in Show award, 19 Group Firsts, 21 Group Seconds, 30 Group Thirds and 28 Group Fourths and one Specialty Best of Breed. He is the sire of at least 15 champion offspring.

Beauregard's daughter, Ch. A.R.E.S. Maah-velous (ex Ch. A.R.E.S. Non-stop of Woodland) is a multiple all-breed Best in Show winner and the top-winning Best in Show bitch in the history of the breed. Ch. A.R.E.S. Happy Hooker O' Landmark was another distinquished bitch, producing ten champion offspring. Ch. A.R.E.S. Magnum Man, UD, (ex. Ch. A.R.E.S. Shortcake),

Ch. Skipalong's Gadget, Sire of thirty-six champion offspring. Gadget was top producing sire of all Non-Sporting dogs in 1972.

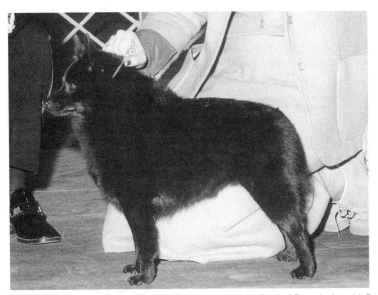

Ch. Padolin's Missle Two of A.R.E.S. This bitch garnered 61 Best of Breed wins, 98 Best of Opposite Sex wins, 36 Group placements, 2 Specialty Best of Breed awards, and 8 Specialty Best of Opposite Sex awards. She was the SCA Top Winning Bitch in 1975, 1976, and 1977.

Booth

Ch. A.R.E.S. Beauregard O Padolin won 1 all-breed Best in Show award, 19 Group Firsts, 21 Group Seconds, 30 Group Thirds, 28 Group Fourths, and 1 Specialty Best of Breed. He is the sire of at least 15 champion offspring.

Graham

owned by Catherine Fliszer, was the SCA Top Obedience Schipperke for 1984 and 1985. He had five High in Trial awards before his untimely death at the age of six.

ABE'S—Active: 1970s/1980s. Owners: Sonny and June Robertson of Virginia. The Robertsons bred and showed Schipperkes on the east coast. Among their breeding were Ch. Abe's Sonju of N'Ciss, Ch. Abe's Tinker Bell of N'Ciss, and Ch. Abe's D'ebony Drac of N'Ciss, all by their foundation brood bitch, Ch. Valkyra Narcissus D'Ebony.

ALGENE—Active: 1930s/1960. Owners: Mr. and Mrs. McNeil of Michigan. The McNeils established one of the foremost Schipperke kennels in the United States during this period by virtue of their length of service and the number of champions they owned or bred.

They started their kennel with several Canadian-bred bitches and the Cali-

Ch. A.R.E.S. Magnum Man, UD, owned by Catherine Fliszar, was the SCA Top Obedience Schipperke for 1984 and 1985. Ch. A.R.E.S. Don Duts, CDX (left), also has won many Obedience awards.

fornia-bred male, Ch. Coltness Little Skipper. Two of their first homebred champions were Ch. Dixie Lee of Algene (a linebred daughter of Ch. Coltness Little Skipper), dam of several champions; and Ch. Dempsey's Black Streak (son of Ch. Dixie Lee of Algene), the sire of champions. An outstanding bitch was Ch. Algene's Chicho Para, who, in her short career, won Best of Breed at Westminster in 1938 and two Non-Sporting Group Firsts, including one in Canada. Sadly, Chicho Para died when less than two years old. Her full sister, Ch. Algene's Chicho Para II was the dam of champions.

Algene's best champion producers during the 1940s and 1950s were Canadian and American Ch. Night Cap of Cal-Ann (Ch. Argun's Howie Boy O'Marward ex Patsy Girl), Ch. Haila's Gallant Pepin (Arlo of Kelso ex Haila of Kelso) and Algene's Maybelle of Anyost. Algene bred numerous champions, two of whom became prominent producers of champions: Ch. Cadet Teddy of Algene (Ch. Top-Marc La Puce of Ochsnerhof ex Ch. Lady Sonia of Algene).

Their most celebrated dog was Am/Can Ch. Night Cap of Cal-Ann, a son of Ch. Argun's Howie Boy O'Marward bred by Caldon Gee (Cal-Ann). Night Cap topped his show career by winning three Group Firsts. He was the sire of five champions. By 1960, Mrs. McNeil retired from all Schipperke activities, leaving a great heritage for the breed in following years.

ALPCRAFT—Active: 1930s/1940s. Owner: Gottlieb Zulliger of Wisconsin. Mr. Zulliger was an active breeder in the early 1930s. Pedigrees indicate his breeding began with a daughter of the Belgian import, Belg. Ch. Boule des Bois Mures. His stud dogs descended primarily from English bloodlines, particularly Alpcraft Robbie, a son of English imports Ch. Royd Robbie and Bette o'the North. Their most noted Schipperkes were Alpcraft Peggy, whose bloodline has descended to the present day; Ch. Alpcraft Pat; and Flickamorru's Kate, a granddaughter of Belg. Ch. Boule des Bois Mures.

ANYOST—Active: 1940s/1950s. Owner: Mrs. Unger. Anyost kennels bred and showed Schipperkes on a limited basis. Their most noted dogs were the champions Ch. LeMay of Anyost (owned by judge Dr. A. A. Mitten) and Ch. Nikki of Algene.

BARCAROLE—Active: 1960s-present. Owner: Douglas H. Wilson of Louisiana. Mr. Wilson has been an active breeder and exhibitor and is also an AKC licensed judge. He has completed titles on a number of Schipperkes, and others of his breeding have been finished by different owners. Mr. Wilson's Schipperkes are strong in the bloodline of the renowned Ch. Klinahof's Marouf A Draco and his foundation bitch was Ch. Prince O'Pal's Asta II.

BEAUMONT—Active: 1940s-late 1950s. Owners: Mr. and Mrs. Robert Snider of Ohio. One of their early bitches was Ch. Algene's Chicho Para II, a dam of champions. Her daughter, Prima Donna of Beaumont, and her granddaughter, Algene's Sali of Beaumont, carried on the tradition by producing champion get of their own. The Sniders owned several other champions, including Ch. Corey Boy of Cal-Ann (Ch. Smithstone Clovis of Kelso ex Judy Girl of Cal-Ann), himself a sire of champions.

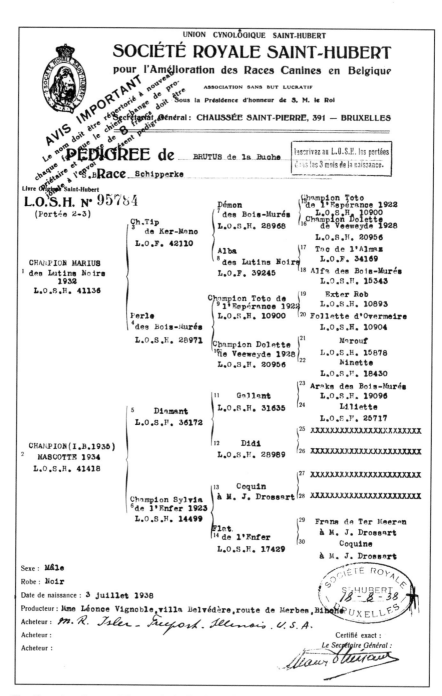

The Export pedigree of Brutus de la Buche, a Belgian Schipperke exported to the United States in 1938. Note that Didi and Coquin on his dam's side have unknown origins. In order to be registered in the United States, the dog was required to have at least a three generation pedigree.

In 1938, Mr. and Mrs. Isler of Illinois imported Brutus de la Buche, a son of Belgian Ch. Marius des Lutins Noirs, and Annette de l'Esperance to the United States. The Islers are pictured on board the ocean liner *Normandie* with their new additions. Brutus is the puppy.

BEALL-JAN—Active: 1950s/1970s. Owner: Dr. Charles Beall of Georgia. During the 1950s, Dr. Beall often had the only Schipperke entries at some of the shows in the Southeast. He also bred a number of champions. His most outstanding dog was Ch. Lo-Lane Lad of Fortune.

BELIQUE—Active: 1970s/present. Owner: Kathy Friedt of Washington. One of her most outstanding winners has been Am. Can. Ch. Roetmop Captain Caius CD, winner of numerous Group placings and sire of champions. Belique Schipperkes have also won numerous titles in Obedience. One of the outstanding Obedience winners from this kennel was Ch. Belique's Glory Seeker, UDT, an outstanding Schipperke performer.

BELLE NOIRE—Active: 1960s/1970s. Owner: Mrs. Jerry Hackney of Oklahoma. Belle Noire Kennels is the breeder of Ch. Belle Noire Nothing Else, owned by the de Sang Bleu kennels. She is the dam of seventeen champion offspring, including Am/Can/Mex Ch. Eatchurheartout de Sang Bleu, a multiple Best in Show winner.

BERESFORD—Active: 1930s/1940s. Owners: Mr. and Mrs. Beresford of California. A Schipperke bearing the Beresford name, Ch. Chou Chou of

Ch. Belique's AWOL From Ni-Kel, CDX. This Schipperke has won 1 all-breed Best in Show, 19 Group Firsts, 26 Group Seconds, 29 Group Thirds, and 22 Group Fourths. He is also a fine working Obedience Schipperke. *Ross*

Beresford, made this championship in 1928. Bold Brigand of Beresford (son of the English import, My Billy Boy), was a popular stud on the West Coast in the 1930s.

BERNIE'S—Active: 1970s/1980s. Owners: Mr. and Mrs. Bernard Ziegler. Their most noted Schipperke, Ch. Bernie's Shadow of Dark Star, won two all-breed Bests in Show in 1974, as well as a number of Best of Breed awards and Group placings. Mr. Zeigler also trained a brace and showed them to many Best Brace in Show wins.

BETTICO—Active: 1970s/1980s. Owners: Mr. and Mrs. D. H. Coulson

Ch. Belle Noire Nothing Else, owned by de Sang Bleu kennels. She is the dam of seventeen champion offspring, including Am/Can/Mex Ch. Eatchurheartout de Sang Bleu, a multiple Best in Show winner.

of Colorado. These Schipperkes strongly manifest Mace breeding. One of their biggest winners was Ch. Lo-Lane Nightwind of Mace.

BITTERSWEET—Active: 1930s/1940s. Owners: Mr. and Mrs. Clarence E. Bittner of Illinois. In addition to some Noirmont Schips, the Bittners acquired Ch. Seeshes Picaro and Ch. Kincot Irette. Although they only showed on a limited basis, this kennel name can be seen in several pedigrees. The Bittersweet name later was used by another Midwest breeder.

BLACKANGEL—Active: 1970s/present. Owner: Doris Giesler of Illinois. Her notable Schipperke, Ch. Black Angel's Casey, UD, completed his championship at two years of age and completed his Utility Dog title at age six.

BLACKJACK—Active: 1970s/present. Owner: Lee Ann Stusnick of Texas. Blackjack Kennels' most outstanding dog has been Ch. Blackjack's Abracadabra (Ch. Kleingaul's B.J.'s Schip in Hand ex Camplaren's Querida, C.D.). Abra was the number four Schipperke bitch in the SCA for 1987 and number eight SCA bitch in 1988. She is a multiple Group placer, including a Group First, and the dam of four champion offspring.

BLUMOON—Active: 1970s/present. Owners: Grant and Anita Fredericks of Washington. Their kennel produced Ch. Blumoon's Notail T O'Nopocin and Ch. Blumoon's BB O'Nipocin and is the home of Am/Can U-CDX Midnight Meadows Cinderella. This bitch has placed in the Non-Sporting group in the United States and Canada and is the dam of ten champion offspring.

BRADERIE—Active: 1970s/present. Owners: Mr. and Mrs. Walter Keating of Florida. Ch. Von Kay's Belgium Baron of Tuff (Ch. Del-Dorel's Tuffite ex Ch. Von Kay's Ima Emma) was the Keatings' most noted dog. He was a multiple Best of Breed winner and had many Group placements. Perhaps his most

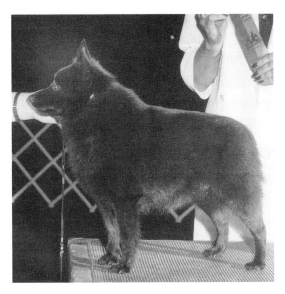

Ch. Blackjack's Abracadabra. "Abra" was the number four bitch in the SCA for 1987 and number eight SCA bitch in 1988. She is a multiple Group placer, including a Group First, and the dam of four champion offspring. *Olson*

outstanding accomplishment occurred at the 1985 Schipperke Club of America Specialty show when he won Best of Opposite Sex at fourteen and one-half years of age! After Mr. Keating's death, Mrs. Keating, who is also an AKC licensed judge, relocated to Fulton, Missouri.

BRAKEN—Active: Mid-1960s/present. Owner: Dolores Arste of New York. Braken kennels is the home of Ch. Braken's Triple Crown, a multiple Group placer. Ms. Arste is also an AKC licensed judge.

BURKE'S—Active: Late 1920's/1940's. Owners: Mr. and Mrs. Louis A. Burke of Rhode Island. The Burkes began exhibiting with Ch. Fortune's Laddy Boy (linebred grandson of Yperland Peter Simon). Laddy won twenty-four Best of Breed awards by the time he was retired. During the early 1930s, the Burkes acquired a number of Schipperkes, some of which were champions, from the elder Mr. A. M. Burke. Among these was his foundation bitch, Yperland Lady Ora Belle (granddaughter of imported My Billy Boy and of Yperland Peter Simon), who deserves mention as the dam of seven champions, an outstanding achievement for any Schipperke bitch. One of her daughters, Ch. Burke's Di-An, placed second in the Non-Sporting Group several times.

The brightest star of this kennel was Ch. Burke's Tarzan (Ch. Veeson of Kelso ex Yperland Lady Ora Belle). Tarzan attained the remarkable record of fifty-nine Best of Breed wins and twenty-three Group placings, including 5 Group Firsts. These were at a time when Group wins were almost nonexistent for the breed. Tarzan also won Best of Breed at Westminster in 1935. Not only was he an outstanding show winner but he also proved his worth by siring a number of champions as well. There were other champions bred by the Burkes prior to the death of Mrs. Burke in 1936.

CAE—Active: 1960s–1970s. Owner: Elizabeth Lafferty of New Jersey. Mrs. Lafferty began exhibiting in the 1960s and completed championships on a number of Schipperkes. Nearly all were descendants of the famous Ch. Dark Star of Cledlo. The best known is Ch. Cae's Arletta, a daughter of Ch. Del-Dorel's Stardom. Arletta did much winning and was SCA Top Winning Bitch for 1968 and tied for that honor in 1969. Ch. Cae's Black Bandit, a son of Ch. Toni's Mark of Dark Star, was a Best of Breed winner with several Group placings. The Cae Kennels were inactive after 1974.

CAL-ANN—Active: 1940s/1950s. Owners: Mr. and Mrs. Caldon Gee. They started Ch. Argun's Howie Boy O'Marward on his noted career. They also bred Am/Can Ch. Night Cap of Cal-Ann and Ch. Corey Boy of Cal-Ann as well as Ch. Black Skipper of Cal-Ann. George Hines owned and showed several Cal-Ann Schipperkes, beginning in 1948 (mostly in Canada) with two sons of Ch. Argun's Howie Boy O'Marward bred by Mr. Caldon Gee.

CAMPLAREN—Active: 1970s/present. Owners: Mr. and Mrs. John Bernhardt of Ontario, Canada. Am/Can Ch. Roetmop Pretty Princess, CD, was the foundation bitch for Schipperkes of the Camplaren kennel, producing many champion get. Ch. Camplaren's Krowning Glory was a winner in the United States and Canada. In 1975 Glory was twice the Best Puppy in Show in Canada at seven months of age. She was also Winners Bitch at the 1976 SCA National Specialty and the Illiana Specialty.

Am/Can Ch. Camplaren's Native Son was ranked as Canada's Top Schipperke in 1980, 1981, 1982, and 1983. He was a Best in Show winner in both the United States and Canada and competed four times in Canada's prestigious "Show of Shows," open only to Best in Show winners. He won the Group at the "Show of Shows" twice. He was also ranked second Non Sporting Dog in Canada in 1980.

Am/Can/Bda Ch. Camplaren's Quite a Winner was a multiple Canadian Best in Show winner and was ranked as one of the top Canadian Schipperkes in 1988 and 1989. Am/Can Ch. Knighttime Banner O'Camplaren was a multiple Best in Show winner in Canada and Group winner in the United States. The Bernhardt children, Stephen and Paul, were very active in Junior showmanship and each won a number of Junior Handling awards.

CARLISLES—Active: late 1940s/1960s. Owners: Mr. and Mrs. Eris Carlisle of Illinois. Although this kennel was established a few years prior to 1950, it was not until the mid-1950's that the Carlisles founded their winning line with the purchase of Ch. Al's Prince Mo of Garner (Ch. Alhambra Victory of Kelso ex Jet-O bloodlines) and Ch. Book's Brat of Jet-O. From this pair came Ch. Carlisle's Whiz Bang, top winning Schipperke for 1955 and sire of six champions. By the 1960s the kennel was inactive.

CANTYMERE—Active: 1950s/present. Owner: Mariou Postgate of British Columbia, Canada. Mrs. Postgate has shown a number of Schipperkes to various titles. Her dogs include Ch. Kleingaul's Fox of Cantymere, CD; Ch. Broomhilda, CDX; Ch. Cantymere Black Cara, CD. She is a licensed judge as well.

CHARR COAL—Active: 1970s/1980s. Owner: Lois Border of Oregon. Mrs. Border has shown in the Northwest and her Charr Coal kennels is the home

Am/Can Ch. Chatelet's Kickoff. This Schipperke's career wins include 2 all-breed Best in Show wins, 10 Group Firsts, 38 Group Seconds, 33 Group Thirds, 28 Group Fourths, and 1 Specialty Best of Breed. He has sired 15 champion offspring to date. *Booth*

of Ch. J. R. Bear Koalapepper and Ch. Charr Coalette Dixie Cup, Am UD, Can CDX. Dixie won many awards in Obedience, including a High in Trial in Canada. This Schipperke also works in a nursing home as an active part of the Pet Therapy program.

CHATELET—Active: 1970s/present. Owners: Thomas and Carol Luke of Indiana. Although the Luke's foundation stud, Ch. Jetstar's Touchdown (Ch. Jetstar's Fringe Benefits ex Jetstar's Short Circuit), was specialed to a number of Group placements, his claim to fame was as a producer. To date, he is the sire of twenty champion offspring, including one multiple Best in Show dog, two SCA Top Ten Schipperkes, at least three Group placers and also Specialty Best of Breed winners. He was also a junior handling dog, helping Lara Luke attain SCA Top Junior Handler for two years.

Am/Can Ch. Chatelet's Kickoff (Ch. Jetstar's Touchdown ex Ch. Chatelet's Eau de Joy) finished his championship as a puppy, undefeated and with multiple Group placements. He was co-owned and handled by Rose Thurston for five years, then Mr. Luke took over. Although campaigned on a fairly limited basis, he placed in the SCA Top Ten in 1983. He continued to win Top Ten honors for eight years. His career includes two all-breed Best in Show wins, 10 Group Firsts, 38 Group Seconds, 33 Group Thirds, 28 Group Fourths and one Specialty Best of Breed. He has sired 15 champion offspring to date.

CHINDE—Active: 1970s/1980. Owners: Greg and Kathleen Barrett, later Kathleen Baker-Gumprecht of California. Her Ch. Kleingaul's Koalette Kutie, co-owned with breeder Kathy (Gaul) Montgomery and Theresa Gaul, was the SCA's Top Winning Schipperke Bitch for 1980. Kathleen Baker-Gumprecht and Kathy Mongomery also owned a team consisting of Ch. Kleingaul's Image Maker, Ch. Kleingaul's Easy Come Easy Go, Ch. Kleingaul's No More Mr.

Ch. Chatelet Gunslinger has several Group placings to his credit.   *Cott/Daigle*

Ch. Kleingaul's Koalette Kutie, a Group winner, was the SCA's Top Winning Schipperke Bitch for 1980. *Mikron*

Ch. Kleingaul's Image Maker, Ch. Kleingaul's Easy Come Easy Go, Ch. Kleingaul's No More Mr. Nice Guy, and Frame's Sharou. This team received a standing ovation at the SCA's 50th anniversary Specialty Show and was campaigned to numerous Best Team in Show awards. *Bergman*

Nice Guy, and Frame's Sharou. This team won a standing ovation at the SCA's fiftieth anniversary Specialty Show and was campaigned to numerous Best Team in Show awards. Ch. Kleingaul's Easy Come Easy Go and Ch. Kleingaul's Image Maker were also a brace and won many Best Brace in Show awards.

CHRISTMAS—Active: 1950s/early 1970s. Owner: Mrs. Willis Gilmore. Mrs. Gilmore began showing in 1955 with Ch. Corinda of Cledlo, a Ch. Dark Star of Cledlo daughter. Corinda produced six champions, including Ch. Christmas Rudolph and Ch. Christmas Eve.

CINDY-KE—Active: 1970s/1980s. Owner: Mary Sue Bynum of California. Mrs. Bynum and her granddaughter, Lori Turner Wilson, owned and campaigned their bitch Ch. Jetstar's Dust Moppe to SCA Top Winning Bitch for 1978 and 1979. Ch. Cindy-Ke's Banjo and Ch. Jetstar's Dust Moppe were shown to multiple Best Brace in Show awards.

CLEDLO—Active: 1947–1970s. Owners: Mr. and Mrs. Howard L. Dietrich of New York. The Dietrichs established their Cledlo Kennels in 1947 with the purchase of Fanchon's Reverie, a daughter of Fanchon of Kelso. Soon afterward, they acquired Alhambra's Victoria of Kelso (Ch. Alhambra Victory of Kelso ex Bellady of Bittersweet) and Ruffian's Soloette (Ch. Black Ruffian ex Ch. Black Rose of Ecloo), both of which earned titles.

In 1947, the Dietrichs purchased Ch. Alhambra Victory of Kelso (Ch. Jason of Kelso ex Ch. Kiska of Kelso), who became the extraordinary foundation stud for Cledlo Kennels. This dog built an enviable record in the show ring, winning numerous Group placings. He was also a significant sire, producing at least twelve champions. Alhambra Victory's line became famous as having produced three Best in Show winners in direct male descent.

Ch. Ruffian's Soloette also did her share by producing several champion offspring. Other Schipperkes bred by Cledlo achieved their championship titles with other owners. One of these was the distinguished multiple Best in Show winner, Ch. Dark Star of Cledlo.

CLOVER DELL—Active: 1970s/present. Owners: Rocky and Bonnie Volpp of Ohio, then Texas. Their kennel was home to Ch. Jetstar's Inner Sanctum, a notable winner.

COLEHAVEN—Active: late 1960s—to mid-1970s. Owners: Mr. and Mrs. Charles Cole of Texas. The Coles started breeding and exhibiting dogs with Lo-Lane and Stardom bloodlines, finishing several champions. The Coles were also active participants in the formation of the Lonestar Schipperke Club, which hosted the 1973 National Specialty. One of the Cole's better-known winners was Am/Can/Mex/Int'l Ch. Mace's Rambler. Ch. Mace's Dallas was Best of the Opposite Sex at the 1973 Specialty.

CULBERTSON, R. E.—Active: 1920s. Mr. Culbertson of Chicago bred and exhibited in the early 1920s. He preferred the larger Schipperke and disliked anything under sixteen pounds. One of his breeding, Broadcast, was a favorite of judge Irene Castle Schlintz. Later, Mr. Culbertson moved to Minnesota, where he kept only a few dogs, and most of his stock then went to the West Coast.

CRANFIELD, GEORGE A.—Active: 1920s/1940s. Mr. Cranfield of California was probably the most active Schipperke breeder on the West Coast during the 1920s. He was not only a breeder and exhibitor, but also an importer, judge, and very prolific writer on the breed. Perhaps the most important dog he owned was the import My Billy Boy who founded a male line through a son, Ch. Coltness Little Skipper. Skipper was the foundation for several successful Midwest kennels of the 1930s. Another English import, Royd Robbie, completed an American championship and was the founder of another, but less prolific, male line which is still in existence. Of his imported bitches, Bette o'the North received much publicity but left little permanent impression on the breed today.

CRYSTALTON—Active: 1970s/present. Owners: Charles and Carol Graham of Alberta, Canada. Their most noted Schipperke has been Am/Can/Bmda Ch. Fairlaur Diablo, an American and Canadian Best in Show winner. Diablo was Canada's top winning Schipperke for the years 1975, 1976, 1977, and 1978.

DALY—Active: 1940s/1950s. Owners: Mr. and Mrs. L. S. Daly. The Dalys were active at Eastern shows during the 1940s and added several champions to their breeding record, including Ch. Daly's Favorite of Algene (Ch. Cadet Teddy of Algene ex Prima Donna of Beaumont). This Schipperke whelped four champions under the Daly banner and one for another kennel.

Another valuable dog the Daly's acquired was Ch. Argun's Howie Boy O'Marward, bred by Fred Gunther. This Schipperke, a son of Ch. Little Black Joe O'Marward, made a worthy contribution to the breed in the many champion offspring he sired both in the Midwest and the East. Two other Daly homebreds deserving of mention were the multiple champion producers, Ch. Daly's Coronet

Ch. Del-Dorel's Stardom garnered numerous Best of Breed wins and 94 Group placings, including 23 Group Firsts, and 9 Best in Show awards. He was SCA Top Winning Schipperke for the years 1960–1964 and top sire with 39 champions. *Frasie*

Jewel (Ch. Daly's Tar-Zan by Tarzan ex Ch. Daly's Jewel from Judy) and Daly's Di-Dee of Di-An, daughter of Ch. Burke's Di-An.

DE BELGIUM—Active: 1970s/1980s. Owner: Patricia Keener of Ohio. Ch. DeBelgium's Adonis was one of the better-known dogs from this kennel and competed in both the conformation and obedience ring with his owner, Anna Belle Boesch.

DEJA-VUE—Active: 1970s/present. Owners: Roger and Jackie Dawson of Illinois. Ch. Black Angel's Casey, UD, is the recent star of Deja-Vue Kennel. He earned 194 and a First Place in the Utility Class while qualifying for the second leg of his UD. In addition to his Obedience degree, as a champion of record, he emphasizes the breed's versatility.

DEL-DOREL—Active: 1950s/1970s. Owners: Mr. and Mrs. Del Lasser of Illinois. They are best known for their homebred Ch. Del-Dorel's Stardom, a Ch. Dark Star of Cledlo son, an extremely influential Schipperke of his day. Besides his numerous Best of Breed wins, he won ninety-four Group placings, including twenty-three Group Firsts and nine Best in Show awards. He was SCA Top Winning Schipperke for the years 1960–1964, inclusive.

Not only the breed's greatest winner of his time, he was also a great sire with thirty-nine champions to his credit. Two of his sons also won Best in Show honors. Del-Dorel Kennels closed completely following the untimely death of Del Lasser in 1971.

DE PATGE—Active: 1950s/1970s. Owner: George B. Hines of Missouri. His first champion was Ch. Black Skipper of Cal-Ann, son of Ch. Argun's Howie Boy O'Marward, in 1952. In the mid-1950s he added Kelso bloodlines from Lo-Lane and Marless Kennels. From this combination Mr. Hines began producing winners and was the breeder of several champions. His best producers were Ch. Gee Bee's Boudwarrier (Ch. Maroufke of Kelso line) and the bitch, Ch. Gee Bee's Hazey Hundy of Keuka, bred by the Hundleys.

DE SANG BLEU—Active: 1970s/present. Owners: Greg, Paul, and Maureen Garrity of California. The Garrity's foundation bitch, Ch. Belle Noir Nothing Else, produced an outstanding record of seventeen champion get for this kennel, including Ch. Eatchurheartout de Sang Bleu ("Jojo").

By the time he was retired, Jojo had amassed 13 all-breed Best in Show awards, 2 national Specialty Best of Breed wins, 310 Best of Breed wins, 58 Group Firsts, 59 Group Seconds, 48 Group Thirds, and 35 Group Fourths. He was the top winning Schipperke in all systems for 1981, 1982, 1983, 1984, and 1985.

Other outstanding de Sang Bleu Schipperkes are Am/Can/Mex Ch. Getitgotitgood de Sang Bleu, a multiple Group winner and placer, and Am/Mex Ch. Gretta de Sang Blue, Group winner and multiple Group placer and the SCA Top Winning Bitch for 1981 and 1982.

DONRHO—Active: late 1950s/1970s. Owners: Mr. and Mrs. Donald Holaday of Indiana. They began showing in 1958, and during the next decade a large number of Donrho Schipperkes were exhibited extensively throughout the

Ch. Del-Dorel's Tuffite. This Schipperke sired fifteen champions, including Ch. Elfe-Mir's Billie Billy Bi-Ho, Ch. Elfe-Mir's A Bounc-En Skipper, Ch. Von Kay's Electra of Tuff and Ch. Von Kay's Belgian Baron of Tuff.

Midwest with many being shown to championships. Their foundation stud was Ch. Walrose Stargin, a Ch. Dark Star of Cledlo son, who was not only shown with success but also sired ten champions. Other Donrho-bred Schipperkes became champions with other owners, and several kennels were founded with Donrho stock. This kennel was disbanded after the death of Mrs. Holaday.

DO-WELL—Active: 1970s/present. Owner: D. K. Walton. The most outstanding dog from this kennel was Ch. Do-Well's Nitro (Ch. Skipalong's Gadget ex. Ch. Wilbet's Merry Mistletoe, UD). "Nitro" won many Best of Breed awards, Group placings, a Specialty win, and a Best in Show. In addition, he was Miss Stephens' (A.R.E.S.) junior handling dog and helped her become the third highest ranked junior handler among all breeds in the United States in 1975, according to the Kennel Review system.

DREAM ON—Active: 1960s/present. Owners: William and Marcia Bailey of Iowa. Dream On Kennels bred their first champion-producing litter in 1968 and since that time have bred and finished championships on nearly one hundred Schipperkes. Dogs of San-Dil breeding formed the base for the Dream On breeding program.

Their most outstanding dog has been Ch. Dream On's One In A Million (Ch. Eatchurheartout de Sang Bleu ex Ch. Dream On's Enchantment), a seventh generation dog of Dream On breeding. "Chance," as he is called, finished his championship undefeated at eight months of age. He then began a show career that is unequaled in the breed. He is the top Schipperke all-breed Best in Show

Am/Can/Mex Ch. Getitgotitgood de Sang Bleu (on left), a multiple Group winner and placer, and Am/Mex Ch. Gretta de Sang Bleu, Group winner and multi-Group placer as well as the SCA Top Winning Bitch for 1981 and 1982. *Yuhl*

winner. His first Best in Show was awarded on January 3, 1987. Since that date he has won this honor a total of fifteen times. He also has won 68 Non-Sporting Group Firsts, 59 Group Seconds, 38 Group Thirds, 20 Group Fourths, and 4 Speciality Best of Breed Awards.

"Chance" also won Best of Breed twice at Westminister Kennel Club, then went on to win a Group Third in 1988 and a Group Second in 1989, making "Chance" the only Schipperke to ever place higher than Group Third and the only Schipperke to place in the Group twice at this prestigious show. In addition, "Chance" is the SCA Top Winning Schipperke for the years 1986, 1987, 1988, 1989, and 1990, and has sired at least ten champion offspring. He was retired with a Best of Breed win from the Veteran Dog class at 8½ years of age at the record breaking 1991 SCA National Specialty Show.

EBON IMP—Active: 1960s/1970s. Owners: Miss R. Benton and Virginia and Nancy Updike of Maryland. One of their top winners was Ch. Ebon Imp Apollo (Ch. Ye Ole Lamplighter of San-Dil, CD ex Ch. Toni's Waltzing Shadow), who captured the Best of the Breed at the Schipperke Club of Greater St. Louis Specialty in 1973.

EBONYSTAR—Active: 1970s/present. Owner: Lynn Brown of California. Ebonystar is the home of Ch. Ebonystar Salute to Sarahtoga, Best of Winners at the 1989 SCA National Specialty and Group placer and multiple Best of Breed winner.

ECLOO—Active: 1938/mid-1950s. Owner: Mrs. Oakley French of Connecticut. Although established in 1938 with the purchase of Fanchon of Kelso

46

Ch. Elfe Mir's Billie Billy Bi-Ho. He was a multiple Best in Show winner and the sire of twenty champions. He was the SCA Top Winning Schipperke in 1973 and 1974. *Ritter*

(Ch. Pepin le Bref of Kelso ex Ch. Claudine of Kelso), Ecloo Kennels became better known in the 1940s for its outstanding Maroufke son, Ch. Black Ruffian, who won over all competition except his sire. By the time of his retirement, Ruffian had amassed some 150 Best of Breed awards and more than 40 Group placings, including two Group Firsts.

Fanchon of Kelso was easily the star bitch of this kennel, producing seven champions in five litters sired by five different studs, a notable feat in her own right. She herself won a five point major the only time she was shown. Two of her champion offspring produced champions; namely, Ch. Black Ruffian and his litter sister, Ch. Fanchon's Dusky Rose. Many other Ecloo champions sired or whelped at least one champion, and the line of Fanchon is still producing champions. This kennel is somewhat unusual in that it based its long-range breeding program on the linebreeding of a strong female line, a practice recommended by various authorities but not too often followed; linebreeding on an outstanding dog is more common. The death of Black Ruffian closed an outstanding chapter for the Ecloo Kennels. After showing a few other Schipperkes to title Mrs. French retired and closed her kennels.

E'LAN—Active: 1970s/present. Owner: Betty Jo Patrick of Washington state. E'lan is the home of Ch. Slyfox E'Lan's Stutz Bear Kat and Ch. Barbil E'Lan's Fortune Teller, dam of nine champions. This kennel also produced Ch. Elan's Yentl, the SCA Top Obedience Schipperke for 1987.

ELFE-MIR—Active: 1970s/1980s. Owner: Effie Meyer of Minnesota. The Elfe-Mir Kennels produced many fine Schipperkes, including the SCA Top

Winning Schipperke of 1973 and 1974, Ch. Elfe Mir's Billie Billy Bi-Ho. Billie was owned by Fran Griggs and Richard Wasserman. He was a multiple Best in Show winner and the sire of twenty champions.

Another Best in Show winner was Ch. Elfe-Mir's a Bounc-En Skipper, co-owned by the Griggs and Sue McFall of Missouri. He was the sire of eighteen champions. Both these Schipperkes were sired by Ch. Del-Dorel's Tuffite, a Stardom son.

EL RU—Active: 1930s/1940s. Owner: Elsie Hoyt of California. She bred from the Belgian bloodlines of Franswold and Kelso.

ETTYHAVEN—Active: 1930s/1940s. Owner: Henrietta Proctor Donnell of New York. Mrs. Donnell was first known for another breed; however, she saw the Kelso dogs at Eastern shows in the late 1920's and became interested in the Schipperke. She borrowed her neighbor's Schipperke, Colas de Veeweyde (imported) owned by Mrs. John Ranson, and started showing him. Thereafter, she acquired Reine Margot of Kelso (daughter of imported Max de Veeweyde) and showed her to a championship. Before Reine Margot's untimely death at two years of age, this little bitch did remarkable winning, placing in the Group many times, winning several seconds and one Group First. Henrietta Donnell owned several other Schipperkes and did some breeding, but never equaled the record of Reine Margot. Her interest in the breed never wavered and she devoted many years of service to The Schipperke Club of America, Inc.

FAIRLAUR—Active: 1950s/1970s: Owner: Fran Hoye of Canada. Am/Can/Bmda Ch. Fairlaur Diablo is both an American and Canadian Best in Show winner. Diablo was Canada's top winning Schipperke for the years 1975, 1976, 1977, and 1978.

FAIRMONT—Active: 1950s. Owner: Mrs. Allen Keally of Knoxville,

Ch. Elfe-Mir's a Bounc-En Skipper, co-owned by the Griggses and Sue McFall of Missouri. He was an all-breed Best in Show winner and the sire of eighteen champions.

Tennessee. Mrs. Keally exhibited in the 1950s and bred and finished a number of champions. The star of this kennel was Ch. Roly Poly of Kelso (Ch. Maroufke of Kelso line), winner of three Group Firsts and the top winning Schipperke for 1953. He also sired five champions.

FARSKANE—Active: 1940s/1950s. Owner: John K. Fasken of Oklahoma. Beginning with Ch. Algene's Fluffy Secrete (Ch. My Frisky Boy ex Ch. Lady Sonia of Algene) he bred her to Ch. Algene's Little Black Joe. Mr. Fasken later purchased and showed to their championships Ch. Smithstone Butcher Boy CD (Ch. Maroufke of Kelso ex Celtic of Kelso) and Ch. Farskane's Happy of Algene, a direct descendant of Ch. Burke's Tarzan. Both dogs won Group placings during their show careers. From these bloodlines have come some present-day champions. After 1961, Mr. Fasken did very little showing and closed his kennel in the late 1960s.

FRAKARI—Active: 1950s–late 1970s. Owners: Fran and Richard Wasserman of New Jersey. The Wassermans owned Ch. Skipalong's Echo, bred by Fran Griggs. Echo was extensively campaigned in the late 1960s. He won many Group placings, including several Group Firsts and was the SCA Top Winning Schipperke for the years 1971 and 1972. Another dog owned by his kennel was the SCA Top Winning Schipperke of 1973 and 1974, Ch. Elfe Mir's Billie Billy Bi-Ho, co-owned by Fran Griggs and Richard Wasserman. Billie was a multiple Best in Show winner and the sire of twenty champions.

FRANSWOLD—Active: 1930s/1940s. Owners: Mr. and Mrs. Frank A. Miller of Oregon. The Miller's started with Kelso stock and began exhibiting extensively. They showed Ch. Petit Poilu of Kelso to a championship. This dog,

Ch. Franswold's Lady Gay was only the second Schipperke in the United States to win the coveted Best in Show at an American all-breed show. This win was achieved from the classes. She was the first breeder/owned Schipperke to make such a win.

along with Zibette of Kelso, Ch. Claudeke of Kelso, and other later additions, formed the foundation of several champion-producing lines in the West.

In 1944, Franswold's Lady Gay won Best in Show at the Portland Kennel Club in Portland, Oregon. This win, on October 21, 1944, under judge Dr. F. P. Miller, marked only the second time in the United States that a Schipperke had won the coveted Best in Show at an American all-breed dog show. Lady Gay earned this win from the classes and thereafter soon became a champion. Another remarkable first established by this feat was that Lady Gay was the first homebred Schipperke to earn such a win.

FREEWOOD—Active: 1970s/present. Owner: Jeri Pabst of California. The outstanding Schipperkes of the Freewood Kennels are Ch. Kleingauls' Brads Teddy Bear (Ch. Brad Crundwell of Jet-O ex Ch. Valkrya Superfox O Kleingaul) a multiple Group winner and placer. Ch. Kleingaul's Spitfir O'Freewood, CDX (Ch. Kleingaul's BJ's Schip in Hand ex Ch. Valkrya Superfox O Kleingaul) is a multiple Group placer and is often competing in Obedience trials on the same day as winning in the conformation ring.

FROSTDALE—Active: 1970s. Owner: Linda Frost, located in Alabama, later in Minnesota. Her most noted Schipperke was Ch. Frostdale Alexander, a son of Ch. Klinahof's Marouf a Draco. Ch. Frostdale Alexander sired seventeen champions and was one of the foundation sires of the Valkyra Kennels.

GERAURA—Active: 1967–1970s. Owners: Mr. and Mrs. Gerald McNally. First located in the Eastern United States, then Canada, and finally California in 1967. Best known of their Schipperkes was Ch. Del-Dorel's Ele-

Ch. Kleingaul's Spitfir O'Freewood, CDX is a multiple Group placer. She has often competed in and placed in Obedience trials and won in the conformation ring on the same day. *Callea*

gante, a Ch. Del-Dorel Stardom son, and Ch. Geraura's Dandi D'Elegante. Both had numerous Bests of Breed and Group placings.

They also successfully campaigned Ch. Skipalong's Que Sera Sera, a Schipperke they co-owned with Frances Griggs. Ch. Holaday's Petite Amanda, dam of Ch. Klinahof's Marouf a Draco, was also owned by the McNallys in her later years.

GERONIMO—Active: 1930s/1940s. Owners: Mr. and Mrs. Cleveland of San Geronimo, California. They were among the breed's ardent devotees during the 1930s, breeding and showing extensively during this period. Geronimo kennels was home to Busybody and later Geronomo Gamin, bred by Mrs. Rand. Both dogs attained their championships. A son of the English import, Ch. Royd Robbie, Gamin sired several champions. In later years the Geronimo kennels became well known for another breed and was no longer associated with Schipperkes.

GLEN KAY—Active: 1960s/1970s. Owner: Josephine Hammer. Her first champion was Ch. Glen Kay's Banshee, a Schipperke that was very well known in his time.

GLENSHAW—Active: 1950s/1970s. Owner: R. W. Snowdon became interested in the breed in the mid-1950s. He exhibited a number of homebred champions. The star of this kennel was Ch. Glenshaw's Starfire (a Ch. Del-Dorel Stardom son. He had a number of Group placings as well as a Best in Show win in 1968.

GRA-BAR—Active: 1970s. Owner: Barbara Gavin. Best known of the Gra-Bar dogs was O. T. Ch. Gra-Bar's Dancing Duchess. This little bitch was the first Schipperke to earn the prestigious title of Obedience Trial Champion after it was offered by the American Kennel Club. In addition, she was the SCA Top Winning Obedience Schipperke for the years 1976, 1977, 1978, and 1979. Sadly, her owner and handler, Barbara Gavin, died in 1979 after a long illness.

GREEN LAKES—Active: 1950s/late 1980s. Owner: Mr. S. Harris of Virginia. His homebred, Ch. Green Lake's Water Boy, was Best of Breed at Westminister in 1975. (See SHERIDAN).

HAPPY TALK—Active: 1980s/present. Owners: Arthur and Marilyn Busse of Tennessee. Their dogs are strongly bred on Ch. Do-Well's Nitro. Their foundation bitch is from Valkyra breeding. Mr. Busse is also an AKC licensed judge.

HARMONY—Active: 1970s/present. Owner: Janette Sanders of Iowa. Am/Can Ch. Roetmop Flemish Fox Am/Can CD (Ch. Roetmop Y-Naught ex Ch. Roetmop Leah) was Harmony's foundation sire. He sired eighteen champions and was the grandsire of thirty-five champions. One of his daughters, Ch. Bess of Harmony (Ch. Roetmop Flemish Fox, CD ex Ch. Belique's Joy to the World) was Best of Breed at the Schipperke Club of Southern California's Specialty Show in 1980, then won Best of Opposite Sex at the SCA National Specialty the next day.

Another outstanding Harmony Schipperke was Ch. Harmony's Heavensent

Am/Can Ch. Roetmop Flemish Fox Am/Can CD was Harmony kennel's foundation sire. He sired eighteen champions and was the grandsire of thirty-five champions.   *Booth*

(Ch. Lynden's Hi'N Mighty ex Ch. Harmony's Carefree Cara Mia). She won many Best of Breed awards and group placings on her way to earning the honor of SCA Top Winning Bitch for 1985 and 1986.

HELART—Active: 1960s. Owners: Mr. and Mrs. C. A. Reinhold of Connecticut. The Reinholds began exhibiting and breeding in the 1960s. They

Ch. Harmony's Heavensent. This bitch won many Best of Breed awards and Group placings and was the SCA Top Winning Bitch for 1985 and 1986.   *Olson*

purchased several Schipperkes which they showed to their title. Their most noteworthy dog was Ch. Helart's Ragamuffin, Best of Breed winner and sire of champions. When the Reinholds retired in the late 1960s, Ragamuffin was returned to his breeder, Mrs. Walter Lake. There, he continued his winning ways and won several Group Firsts.

HEMSHELL—Active: 1910s/1950s. Owner: Joseph Hemshell. Beginning around 1910, Mr. Hemshell imported and exhibited a number of Schipperkes, including, in 1917, the English import Ch. Linden Luck. This dog was undefeated wherever shown. Linden Luck was described by one early writer as having been the best Schipperke brought to America during the prewar years.

A later champion owned and shown by Mr. Hemshell was Ch. My Frisky Boy. Mr. Hemshell continued to be active as a breeder and exhibitor until his death in April 1952.

HOBBITON—Active: 1970s/present. Owner: Laura Nichols of Texas. Ch. Hobbiton's Tinuvial of L.C., CDX, won Best of Opposite Sex and Best of Winners at the 1985 Lone Star Specialty (Texas) for a five-point major. She also won three class placements in the Novice B class while earning her CD title. In 1987, this bitch was ranked as the number five Schipperke in Obedience by the SCA. She also raced for several years with the "Tail-less Wonders Scent Hurdle Team," made up of Schipperkes and Welsh Corgis. The team raced for the first time in the 1986 Gaines Classic and placed fourth. They continued to race for several years, appearing in the Astrohall series of shows and at several National Specialties.

HOLLIDAZE—Active: 1970s to early 1980s. Owner: Barbara Holl of Indiana. Her outstanding Schipperkes were Ch. Skipalong's When You Say Bud, sire of twenty-three champions and Ch. Hollidaze Taster's Choice.

HOLLYBEAR—Active: 1970s/1980s. Owners: Richard and Laura Smith. The Smiths best-known dog was Ch. Hollybear's Warlock. He was shown to many Best of Breed wins in Califonia and several Group placings.

HOLLY RIDGE—Active: 1970s. Owner: Marilyn Boland of South Carolina. One of her outstanding bitches was Ch. Toni's Little Bit O' Dixie.

HONEY LANE—Active: 1950s/1970s. Owners: Mr. and Mrs. Laurence Figge of New Mexico. The Figges became actively interested in breeding and exhibiting while they lived on the East Coast in the 1960s. Their first Schipperke Ch. Del-Dorel's Achates, a Ch. Del-Dorel's Stardom daughter, was dam of seven champions. The Figges campaigned an Achate's son, Ch. Honey Lane's Barry FW, to many Best of Breeds wins and Group placings, including several Group Firsts, They also campaigned a team and a brace to many Best Brace and Best Team in Show awards. Later they moved their kennel to New Mexico, where they continued breeding and showing. A bitch of their breeding, Ch. Honeylane's Dare Non Play Girl, was the SCA Top Winning Schipperke Bitch in 1973. The Figges retired from showing in the late 1970s.

IMNA—Active: 1910s/1930s. Owner: Minnie Bullock first lived on the East Coast, then moved to California. She was active on the West Coast for some years following World War I and claimed to have introduced Schipperkes to California when she moved there with twelve dogs. In the East, the Imna Schips were shown quite extensively. Their descendants may still exist on the West Coast, but none are known to remain in the East.

JA-MAR—Active: 1950s/1970s. Owners: Mr. and Mrs. D. J. Martin of Missouri. They began showing Schipperkes in the 1950s with Lindette's Sugar Plum, a granddaughter of Ch. Lo-Lane Othello of Kelso, and Lindette's Teddy Bear, her half brother and a son of Ch. Nahiman Raven. Both completed their championships and produced several champion get. The Martins campaigned Teddy Bear to numerous wins with Group placings, including two Group Firsts. Teddy Bear's son, Ch. Ja-Mar's April Storm, garnered many Group placings. A Storm daughter, Ch. Ja-Mar's Fire Dancer, was co-owned by Mrs. Martin and Mrs. J. V. Northwood. Dancer did considerable winning, including capturing a Group First. She was also SCA Top Winning Schipperke Bitch for 1967.

JET-O—Active: 1930s/1970s. Owners: Mr. and Mrs. Roy C. Henre of Indiana. Jet-O began with two bitches, Belle of Kelso and Bambina of Kelso, both producing three champions each. Bambina became famous when she whelped eight puppies in one litter. Two became champions. Jet-O's first champion, finished in 1936, was Ch. Captain Max of Kelso. Max founded a champion-producing line for this kennel.

A Kelso bitch, which the Henres showed to her championship, was Ch. Jet-O Doleen of Kelso, a dam of champions. Jet-O kennels bred a number of champions during the 1930s and were prominent exhibitors throughout the Midwest. During the war and postwar years of the 1940s, Jet-O kennels persevered in breeding, showing extensively throughout the Midwest, and establishing itself as one of the foremost Schipperke kennels in the United States. Many champions were added to its distinguished roster.

Their wartime star was Ch. Imp of Jet-O, who came from the classes to win a Group First at a Michigan show in 1941. Soon afterwards, Imp added the championship title to his name. Ch. Ace High of Jet-O, grandson of Ch. Maroufke of Kelso, did some nice winning with several Group placings to his credit. He sired several champions.

Jet-O kennels' great sire was Ch. Smithstone Clovis of Kelso (Ch. Maroufke of Kelso ex Ch. Clochette of Kelso), a Schipperke Mr. and Mrs. Henre acquired from Smithstone Kennels and showed to his championship. Ch. Dusky Queen of Jet-O, a descendant of Jet-O's foundation bitch, Bambina of Kelso (Ch. Henri Jaspar of Kelso ex Dusky Lady of Jet-O), added further laurels to this kennel with her champion offspring. In the 1950s, Jet-O kennels became virtually inactive. They sold most of their dogs and retired to the West Coast. Mrs. Henre died a few years later, and Mr. Henre became semi-retired for a time.

Carol Hudkins had done some breeding in California prior to the 1950s, and had finished several champions. In 1959, Mr. Henre and Mrs. Hudkins were married, and the renowned Jet-O Kennels was reborn with stock from both kennels. They also purchased several dogs in the midwest. The Jet-O Kennels continued their activities with many Schipperkes finishing championships.

Their best known Schipperke at that time was Walrose Honey's Belgian Boy, sire of nine champions. He was bred by Walrose Kennels out of a Jet-O bred champion bitch from the Ch. Dusky Queen of Jet-O family. His son, Ch. Bobo of Jet-O was a winner in the early 1960s and a sire of champions. Another son, Ch. Jolly Jinks of Jet-O, earned his title and won two Group Firsts under Fran Griggs' ownership.

One of the last Jet-O winners was Ch. Skipalong's Charcoal Kid, son of Ch. Del Dorel's Stardom and Ch. Whodunit of Jet-O. Ch. Christmas Eve was their final top-producing matron. She whelped eight champion progeny.

JETALL—Active: 1960s/present. Owner: Betty Witt of California. Mrs. Witt purchased Ch. Black Power of Jet-O, Ch. Maid Special of Jet-O, and Little Cuddler of Jet-O and exported all three to Australia in 1970. These three Schipperkes were the first American-bred Schipperkes to be exported to that country.

Ch. Black Power of Jet-O became one of Australia's foundation sires. His son, Ch. Sunnyslopes Jet Set Joe, bred by Amy Cunich, was the first Schipperke in Australia to win a Best in Show. His daughter, Jeto Black Power Charr, was exported to New Zealand in 1976. Not only did this bitch gain her CDX in Obedience, but her daughter, Ch. Westgarth Janah Danski, made history by winning Best Junior in Group at the New Zealand National Dog Show in 1980. Betty Witt later returned to America with Ch. Black Power of Jet-O and remains active in breeding and exhibiting.

JETSTAR—Active: 1960s/present. Owners: Shirley Kornegay and Joie Kornegay Chandler. Jetstar kennels was established in California in the mid-1960s, combining the bloodlines of Kelso, Honey Lane, Jet-O, Notoow, Starbrook, San Dil, Cae, Toni, and others to form its own line.

Ch. Jetstar's Touchdown is the sire of 20 champion offspring, including 1, multi-Best in Show dog, 2 SCA Top Ten Schipperkes, at least 3 Group placers and Specialty Best of Breed winners.

Carter

An outstanding Jetstar dog was Ch. Jetstar's Command Performance, the SCA Top Winning Schipperke for 1978. Co-owned with Mr. and Mrs. William Raines, Ch. Jetstar's Command Performance won numerous Best of Breed awards, including Specialty Bests of Breed. He was also a multiple all-breed Best in Show winner.

Another outstanding winner was Ch. Jetstar's General Custard, owned by Rose Thurston of New Orleans. Ch. Jetstar's Wishful Wynken was SCA Top Winning Bitch in 1970. The 1971 SCA Top Winning Bitch was Ch. San-Dil's Poppy, co-owned by the Kornegays and Ruth Dilly. The 1972 SCA Top Winning Bitch was Ch. Jetstar's Dhu Drop, and the 1973 SCA Top Winning Bitch was Ch. Honey Lane's Dare Non Play Girl, co-owned by the Kornegays and Elizabeth Figge. Ch. Jetstar's Dust Moppe was the SCA Top Winning Bitch in 1978 and 1979. Ch. Jetstar's Dhu Point has sired sixty champions, making him the breed's greatest producing sire.

KELSO—Active: 1920s/1954. Owners: F. Isabel Ormiston and her sister, Clara Ormiston. Over the years, Kelso kennels built up an unequaled record and reputation, having bred or owned approximately one hundred Schipperke champions. Many successful kennels in the United States today have been founded on Kelso Schipperkes. Isabel Ormiston imported her first Schipperke bitch, Flore de Veeweyde, from Belgium in 1924. The following year she imported her foundation stud, Max de Veeweyde, who became the first of many Kelso champions. During the next twenty years, the Ormistons continued to import Schipperkes from Belgium, including several class or championship certificate winners in that country. Among the most important of these were: Gallant of Kelso, Frida des Violettes of Kelso, Bebe de Ter Meeren of Kelso, Belg. Ch.

Imported Ch. Nonette de Veeweyde of Kelso, owned by Kelso Kennels.

Ch. Maxke of Kelso

Dolette de Veeweyde of Kelso, her daughter Fr. Ch. Celtic des Bois Mures, Nonette de Veeweyde of Kelso, and Garce de Veeweyde of Kelso. Bebe, Celtic, Nonette, and Garce all became American champions. Other noteworthy Kelso dogs were: Ch. Reine Claude of Kelso, producer of eleven champions; Ch. 'Ti Noir of Kelso, sire of at least ten champions; Ch. Marouf of Kelso; Ch. Maxke of Kelso; Ch. Monsieur Puce of Kelso; Ch. Cramique of Kelso; Ch. Ricaduena of Kelso; Ch. Claudine of Kelso; Ch. Arlette of Kelso; Nonny of Kelso; and Ch. Minette of Kelso, whose picture was acclaimed by Belgian authorities of her time the ideal silhouette for the breed.

Kelso Kennels remained active in breeding and showing during the war years and beyond. In spite of the dominance of Ch. Maroufke of Kelso during the 1940s, this kennel produced and exhibited many other valuable Schips. In 1941, Ch. Cramique of Kelso won the Non-Sporting Group at the Lackawanna Kennel Club show in Pennsylvania. Ch. Jason of Kelso won this same honor in 1948. In addition, Jason was an excellent stud and produced many champion offspring. Other outstanding champion producers at Kelso during this period were the dogs: Ch. Roland of Kelso, Ch. Maquis of Kelso, Othello of Kelso, Bobylo Fils of Kelso; and the bitches: Ch. Erzulie of Kelso, Ch. Clochette of Kelso, Rockledge Porty O'Marward, Celtic of Kelso, and Lady Haila of Kelso. Many were descendants of the outstanding Ch. Maroufke of Kelso, and their names are seen in many present-day pedigrees.

The peerless Ch. Maroufke of Kelso made his appearance just before the 1940s. During the war years, his incomparable influence began to be felt upon the breed. He was the grandson of the Ormistons' original imported pair, and his quality was acknowledged by Belgian as well as American authorities of his day. By the time he was retired, Maroufke had won fifty Best of Breed awards,

A rare photograph of F. Isabel Ormiston showing Ch. Maroufke of Kelso to Best of Breed.

including one at Morris and Essex in 1939 over a record-setting forty-nine entries. He earned five wins at Specialties and an incomparable five Bests of Breed at Westminster. He also won a number of Group placings.

Though a top winner during his show career, Maroufke's greatest contribution to the breed was in the high quality of the progeny he sired. This Schipperke

Ch. Sheshe's Cleopatra, owned by Kelso Kennels.

Frances Isabel Ormiston's obituary, which appeared in 1954. Her death brought to an end the long and successful era of Kelso Kennels.

59

left a marked influence on breed type, as shown by his record of thirty-two champion progeny. The number of champion descendants traceable to Maroufke is so large that they have never yet been counted. Indeed, *nearly every Schipperke attaining championship status in the United States today descends from Maroufke*. Thus, Ch. Maroufke of Kelso holds a most unique place in the Schipperke Hall of Fame.

Kelso Kennels started the 1950s by completing the championship of Othello of Kelso II, closely bred on Ch. Maroufke of Kelso. Othello II did much winning, earning the title of SCA Top Winning Schipperke of 1952. Also in 1952, Isabel Ormiston imported two Schipperkes from England, all outcrosses for her Belgian bloodlines. One, Monty of Sebring of Kelso, attained his American championship. It was a shock to the Schipperke world when Miss Ormiston died in early 1954, leaving a void in the Schipperke fancy in the United States.

KIMARA—Active: 1970s/1980s. Owner: Mike de Ruyter of California. Mr. de Ruyter was an active Schipperke enthusiast and was instrumental in the formation of the Schipperke Club of Northern California in 1973. His Kimara Schips were strong in Jet-O blood. His most outstanding winner has been Ch. Easter Parade of Jet-O (Ch. Guard All of Jet-O ex Skipalong's Chim Chimini).

KINCOT—Active: 1930s/1940s. Owner: Mr. J. C. Kingsley of Illinois. Mr. Kingsley started his kennel with Kelso dogs and Belgian imports in the late 1920s and showed regularly until he retired from breeding in 1935. He was one of the founding members of The Schipperke Club of America, Inc. One of his breeding, Ch. Kincot Irette, attained championship status while owned by Dr. S. E. Ochsner. Kincot can still be seen in some extended pedigrees, particularly those dogs descending from the Ch. Lady Portia of Kelso, Ch. Roly Poly of Kelso, and Ch. Buzz of Kelso.

KLEINGAUL—Active: 1960s/present. Owners: Richard and Kathy (Gaul) Montgomery of California. Kleingaul kennels' foundation stud dog was Ch. Brad Crundwell of Jet-O, the winner of several Group placements, including Group Firsts. Brad was also a junior handling dog for Mrs. Montgomery's daughter, Theresa. Together they won many junior handling awards and qualified for Westminister. Theresa became the winner of SCA's first Top Junior Handler award. Brad was the sire of several champions, including Ch. Kleingaul's BJ's Schip in Hand, himself the sire of ten champion offspring. Ch. Kleingaul's Koalette Kutie, a Group winner, co-owned with Theresa Gaul and Kathleen Baker-Gumprecht, was the 1980 SCA Top Winning Schipperke Bitch. Mrs. Baker-Gumprecht and Kathy Mongomery also owned a team which won numerous Best Team in Show awards. Their brace also won many Best Brace in Show Awards. (See CHINDE).

Kleingaul acquired Ch. Valkyra Superfox O'Kleingaul (Ch. Skiplong's Billy Bon Howdy Do ex Ch. Valkyra Skip T'My Lou D'Evanz) in the late 1970s. She became the dam of twelve champion offspring. Her daughter, Ch. Kleingaul's Foxfire, won multiple Group placings including several Group Firsts.

Ch. Kleingaul's Foxfire, a multiple Group winner with other Group placings. Foxfire was SCA Top Winning Bitch for 1983 and 1984.
Lidster

Foxfire was SCA Top Winning Bitch for 1983 and 1984. Kleingaul's Sara Lee, CDX, was the SCA Top Winning Obedience Schipperke for 1989 and 1990.

KLINAHOF—Active: 1950s/1970s. Owners: Dr. and Mrs. M. J. Mills of Illinois. Their most outstanding Schipperke was Ch. Klinahof's Marouf A Draco (Ch. Del-Dorel's Stardom ex Ch. Holaday's Petite Amanda) owned by Dean J. D. Jones. Draco was shown to his title under the ownership of Toddie and Houston Clark and then campaigned by Mr. Jones. Draco's record through the 1970s showed more than 250 Best of Breeds, and 131 Group placements, including fifty Group Firsts and twelve Best in Show wins. He was the SCA Top Winning Schipperke for 1969 and 1970. He was also an outstanding producer, siring forty champions, tying for top producing Non-Sporting sire in 1971.

KNIGHTTIME—Active: 1970s/present. Owner: Judy Wells of New York. This kennel is the home of Ch. Knighttime Shining Star, Can TD; and Am/Can Ch. Landmark's Diplomat of Hi-Line, CD, Can TD.

KNOTTY KNOLL—Active: 1970s/present. Owner: Anne K. Smith. She was the breeder of Ch. Knotty Knoll Kornerstone, Best of Breed winner at the Colonial Schipperke first Specialty show, held in 1990.

LANDMARK—Active: 1970s/present. Owner: Doris Hearing of Missouri. Landmark has bred many champions, all strong in Stardom blood. Outstanding Landmark producers include Ch. Landmark's Duffy McFall, the sire of twenty-seven champions and Ch. Landmark's Disco Inferno, the sire of seventeen champions.

Their top producing bitches include Ch. A.R.E.S Happy Hooker O Landmark, the dam of ten champions; Ch. Landmark's Double D of Hi Line, the dam of nine champions, Ch. Landmarks SS Dani Walton, the dam of ten champions, and Ch. Landmarks's Moss Rose, the dam of eight champions.

Landmark is also the home of a Best in Show winning bitch, Ch. Landmark's Candid Glory.

LEARJET—Active: 1980s/present. Owner: Margie Brinkley of Oregon. Learjet's most noteworthy Schipperkes to date include Ch. Jetstar's Nosegay of Dream On (Ch. Jetstar Top Hat and No Tails ex Jetstar's Highlight), the dam of six champion offspring; and her daughter, Learjets's Black Irish Lass (Ch. Knight Watch's Jeremiah ex Ch. Jetstar's Nosegay of Dream On). The latter bitch won an Obedience High in Trial over fifty-six other dogs when she was only fourteen months of age.

LI-JAN—Active: 1980s/1989. Owner: Vivian Nunnally of California. Mrs. Nunnally trained dogs for more than thirty years when she became interested in Schipperkes. One of her Schipperkes, a bitch named Ch. Magic Kachina Doll of Li-Jan (Ch. Spindrift Sarahtoga ex. Ch. Li-Jan's Black Magic of Jet-O, CDX) co-owned with Judy Proulx, went High in Trial with a score of 199½ at the prestigious Beverly Hills Kennel Club on June 23, 1983. This completed her third leg of her CD title. Sadly, Vivian died in 1989.

LO-LANE—Active: 1950s/1970s. Owner: Helen Johnson of Missouri. One of the recipients of the Kelso dogs after the death of Isabel Ormiston was the Lo-Lane Kennels. This kennel began with Jet-O dogs, taking on several from that kennel when the Henres retired to the West. After acquiring the Kelso dogs, Lo-Lane began exhibiting extensively, finishing numerous champions in the 1950s. The first homebred champion, Ch. Lo-Lane Donette, and Ch. Lo-Lane Othello of Kelso, son of Ch. Othello of Kelso II, both finished their titles in three five-point shows within one week—a very rare and unusual accomplishment. Othello sired several champions.

Their star was Ch. Lo-Lane Michele who won a Group First in 1957. Ch. Lo-Lane Hi-Fidelity, owned by Bruce Lowe, also from Springfield, was a Ch. Dark Star of Cledlo grandson and did much winning in the 1950s, including 3 Group Firsts. Another noteworthy dog was Ch. Lo-Lane Lad of Fortune.

LUTINS NOIR—Active: 1940s/1950s. Owners: Mr. and Mrs. Edward G. Jones. The Lutin Noir kennel began in 1943 with the purchase of Smithstone Son of Clovis (Ch. Smithstone Clovis of Kelso ex Ch. Petite Alka's Nylon) and soon after acquired Smithstone La Rita (Ch. Hannibal of Kelso ex Ch. Smithstone Margette). Both were shown to championships. La Rita did her owners proud by making a record of eleven Best of Breed wins, twelve Best Opposite Sex wins, and seven Group placings before her early death at three years of age. They also owned and showed her sister, Ch. Smithstone La Margo.

LYNDEN—Active: 1970s–present. Owners: Mr. and Mrs. Glen Mulherin of Iowa. Ch. Lynden's Fashion Plate, dam of ten champions, Ch. Lynden's Citation, sire of twenty-nine champions; and Ch. Lynden's Hi Hope of Skipalong, sire of thirteen champions, all contributed to the Lynden legacy.

MACE—Active: 1960s. Owners: Mr. and Mrs. Vernon Mace of Kansas. Their best-known dog was Ch. Mace's Rambler, sire of several champion offspring as well as an American, Mexican, Canadian, Bermudian, and International Champion.

MARDECK—Active: 1980s/present. Owner: Marnie Layng of Ontario, Canada. Am/Can Ch. Mardeck's Danae Odae and Am/Can Ch. Mardeck's Rookie Diplomate assist their breeder/owner in her work rehabilitating psychiatric patients. The Schipperkes seem to understand their patients needs and treat each patient with quiet manners and patience.

MARKIF—Active: 1950s/1960s. Owner: Dr. Mark Skiff, Jr., of Oregon. When exhibiting their dogs at various shows in the West, the Franswold Kennels had interested others in the breed, including Dr. Skiff. He founded Markif Kennels on the bloodlines of Franswold and Kelso champions. His first champion was Ch. Franswold's Dominee of Kelso, a dog which won a number of Group placings during his show days. Dr. Skiff completed championships on numerous Schipperkes.

MARLESS—Active: 1940s/1950s. Owner: Leslie T. Kinney of Connecticut. She began showing after she purchased Prince Haile of Kelso, and she soon attained his championship. A son of the great Ch. Maroufke of Kelso, Prince Haile also won a number of Group placings, and was the sire of champions. The principal foundation bitch of this kennel was Ch. Erzulie II of Kelso, a daughter of Ch. Jason of Kelso and Ch. Erzulie of Kelso, who brought honor to Marless by winning First in the Non-Sporting Group from the classes at Batavia, New York, in 1948. Other foundation Schipperkes at Marless were Ch. Oscar of Kelso (Ch. Maquis of Kelso ex Riquette of Kelso) and Ch. Doletta of Kelso (Ch. Jason of Kelso ex Ch. Erzulie of Kelso). When Kelso Kennels closed, Mrs. Kinney received a number of Kelso dogs, including Ch. Fils of Kelso, a 1955 Specialty

BREED and OBEDIENCE CHAMPIONS   ALL REGISTERED WITH AMERICAN KENNEL CLUB
from the

MAY-HE-CO SCHIPPERKE KENNELS

Beverly Hills, California   Malibu, California

"Jones Pays the Freight"

A 1951 advertisement for May-He-Co Kennels owned by Mr. and Mrs. Carlton Jones of California. Note the four non-black Schipperkes. Mr. Jones embraced the breeding of colored Schipperkes, in direct opposition to Isabel Ormiston's promotion of the all-black Belgian Schipperke.

63

winner. This kennel also bred champions owned by others including Ch. Marless Beau Brummel, UD.

MAY-HE-CO—Active: 1940s/1960s Owners: Mr. and Mrs. Carlton Jones of California. The Joneses acquired their first Schipperke in 1943 but did not begin showing until 1946. An outstanding dog bred by Mrs. John Conway from her noted Ch. Dickon of Kelso, Linarm earned his championship title in a few weeks.

Their initial success spurred Mr. and Mrs. Jones to take up breeding and showing of Schipperkes and soon the May-He-Co name was seen consistently at California shows. Ch. Linarm followed in his sire's footsteps by producing numerous champion offspring, surpassing the record of his sire. A bitch, Chloette of Belvoir, daughter of the outstanding producer Ch. Jason of Kelso, contributed to the breed by producing several of the champions sired by Ch. Linarm, all bearing the May-He-Co prefix. Thus, from two top-producing Kelso bloodlines, the May-He-Co champion lines were developed. From these lines the Joneses trained a brace and team which won many Best Brace and Best Team in Show awards.

The kennel then added outside bloodlines that introduced color-producing genes into its breeding stock. It publicly stated its use of non-black Schipperkes for breeding, contending this was necessary for the continued progress of the breed. A few Schipperke breeders followed the example.

A furious controversy with the Schipperke Club of America, Inc., and Isabel Ormiston ensued and Carlton Jones was dropped from the membership roster of the SCA. He then spearheaded a movement to organize a nationwide breed club in opposition to the parent club. The American-Belgian Schipperke Club, Inc., was founded in 1951. It appeared that its intent was to promote the breeding of non-black Schipperkes. In response, The Schipperke Club of America, Inc., amended the breed Standard in 1959 (approved by AKC) to state clearly the disqualification of any Schipperke of a color other than solid black. Both May-He-Co kennels and the American-Belgian Schipperke Club are no longer active.

MEADOWWOOD—Active: 1950s/1970s. Owners: Mr. and Mrs. Bill McFall, of Iowa and then Missouri. During this time they completed at least seven dogs and are best known for Ch. Cleo's Charcoal Baby, who tied for SCA Top Winning Schipperke Bitch for 1966; Ch. Black Velvet of Ashur, a Group winner; and Ch. Elfe Mir's A Bounc-En Skipper and Ch. Meadowwood's Gimmick, both of whom were all-breed Best in Show Winners.

MENG—Active: 1950s/1971. Owners: J. Lipscomb and P. Wren of Virginia. They began exhibiting regularly in the mid-1960s and finished a number of champions. Mr. Lipscomb's Ch. Blacbarris Oky of Marlamac had numerous wins. The kennel's champion-producing matron was Ch. Meng's Honore Glory. Meng Kennels was disbanded following the death of Mr. Lipscomb in 1971.

NAHIMAN—Active: 1939 to 1955. Owner: Katharine Wellman of Massachusetts. After seeing two Schipperkes in a local Obedience class, Miss Wellman

64

A "birthday card" announcing the one year anniversary of the American Belgium Schipperke Club started by Carlton Jones. This club was active for a time but does not exist today.

became interested in the breed and in 1939 bought her first Schipperke, Menelik of Kelso, and trained him in Obedience. This dog not only acquired his CDX degree but was the first of his breed to pass a Tracking Test.

At first, Miss Wellman was primarily interested in Obedience but through Menelik she also became interested in conformation shows and gained a number of championship points before Menelik had to be retired because of a weak heart. Her next Schipperke, Kelso's Amaryllis, was shown to her championship. Another purchase was Nahiman's Ajuga (Titi of Kelso ex Ch. Queen Alka), bred by Mrs. Daudelin, who earned several Obedience degrees including the TD title. Ajuga further proved her value by producing champions, including Nahiman's first homebred, Ch. Nahiman's Cockade, a son of Ch. Maroufke of Kelso. In turn, Cockade sired more Nahiman champions. Other Schipperkes which Miss Wellman purchased and showed to their titles were Ch. Nahiman's Jasmin CDX (Ch. Jason of Kelso ex Ch. Erzulie of Kelso) and Ch. Lili Marlene of Kelso (Ch. Maquis of Kelso ex Ch. Riquette of Kelso).

NANHALL—Active: 1970s/present. Owners: T. Hall and Frances Keyes of North Carolina. The star bitch of this kennel is Ch. Nanhall's Million Dollar Baby.

NOIRMONT—Active: 1930s/1980s. Owners: Mr. and Mrs. Rene Isler of Illinois. One of the first bitches at Noirmont was Alpcraft Peggy, a granddaughter of the English import, Ch. Linden Luck, and of the Belgian import, Belgian

An advertisement for Ch. 'Ti Bonhomme of Kelso, owned by the de Noirmont Kennels from the pre-World War II era. Note the $25 stud fee.

Ch. Boule des Bois Mures. Alpcraft Peggy had won fourteen championship points, including both majors, and had at least one Group placing to her credit when the Islers discontinued exhibiting.

Noirmont Kennels bred successively to studs of Belgian blood. Their champion males, Gilles of Kelso and 'Ti Bonhomme of Kelso, were added for a quality stud force. In 1938, the Islers imported Brutus de la Buche, a son of Belgian Ch. Marius des Lutins Noirs, and Annette de l'Esperance, a daughter of Marius who was in whelp to her sire. The resulting litter included a male, T and T de Noirmont, later acquired by Kelso Kennels.

NOR-LO-CREST—Active: 1950s/1960s. Owners: Mr. and Mrs. Norvil Roberts. Their foundation bitch, Ch. Lo-Lane Viola of Kelso, made an outstanding show record with many Group placings and a Group First. She also produced champions. Her son, Ch. No-Lo-Crest's Mighty Moe, had an even greater show record with four Group Firsts. Moe was the SCA Top Winning Schipperke of 1959. This kennel produced several other champions but closed after Mr. Roberts died in the 1960s.

O'MARWARD—Active: 1930s/1950s. Owners: Mr. and Mrs. C. H. Yates of Illinois. Three of the Yates' better-known dogs were Ch. Top-Marc La Puce of Ochsnerhof and their homebreds, Ch. John Alden O'Marward and Ch. Little Black Jo O'Marward, Best of Breed winner of the first Illiana Schipperke Club Specialty. The Yates also bred Ch. Argun's Howie Boy O'Marward and Rockledge Porty O'Marward, a bitch who produced four Kelso champions and established a valuable champion-producing female family.

PADOLIN—Active: 1960s/1980s. Owners: Dr. and Mrs. Donald Lingard of Illinois. Frequent exhibitors in the Midwest, one of their stars was Ch. Palodin's Mountain Boy (Ch. Fairlaur Cameo's Sunny ex Ch. Roetmop Aveline). Dr. Lingard, a veterinarian, has been a frequent contributor of articles to the SCA Bulletin on Schipperke health and anatomy.

PERKIE'S—Active: 1970s/present. Owner: Hazel Perkins of Connecticut. One of her most noteworthy dogs was Ch. Perkie's Piccolo Pete, a multiple Group placer.

PINEHILL—Active: 1950s/1970s. Owner: Mrs. N. F. Miller of Arizona. Her dog, Ch. Pine Hill's Indigo Bill, became the fourth Schipperke to win an all-breed Best in Show award, and went on to become the first Best in Show winning Schipperke to earn an Obedience title.

PLAYMATE—Active: 1950s/1970s. Owner: Mrs. L. W. Hughes of California. Mrs. Hughes founded Playmate Schipperke Kennels in the 1950s. Her first champion was Ch. Naughty Lady of Shady Lane, CDX, whom she bred to the Best in Show winner, Ch. Pine Hill's Indigo Bill, CD. From these and others she bred several champions and some of these dogs earned Canadian and Mexican titles as well.

PRINCE O'PAL'S—Active: 1950s/1973. Owner: Violet Baird of New York. She began exhibiting in the early 1950s with Schipperkes acquired from Mr. and Mrs. Daly. She finished numerous champions. In the 1960s she purchased May-He-Co's Riki Ricardo and showed him to his championship. Ricardo sired four champions, and a bitch of her breeding, Prince O'Pal's Asta, produced five champions.

RAND—Active: 1920s/1930s. Owner: Mrs. E. Rand of California. Mrs. Rand bred Ch. Samarand, his sister Ch. Demi Tasse, and Ch. Kim. She was also the breeder of Ch. Wallyrand, a dog owned by Grace Wallace. Mrs. Wallace claimed that Ch. Wallyrand was undefeated in the breed.

REE-DAW—Active: 1960s/1980s. Owners: Mr. and Mrs. R. F. Kent of Tennessee. The Kents began breeding and exhibiting using the Ree-Daw prefix. Their Schipperkes were of San-Dil descent, with a great-grandson of Ch. Maroufke of Kelso as foundation stud. The first Ree-Daw champion was shown to that title by ten-year-old Dawn Kent. Mr. Kent was instrumental in helping the Schipperke Club of America revise *The Official Book of the Schipperke* in 1976. Among the Schipperkes they bred was Ch. Ree-Daw's Foxie Chick (Ch. Do-Well's Nitro ex Ch. Allegra of Ree-Daw).

RIALTA—Active: Late 1970s/present. Owners: Al and Rita Tays of Connecticut. Ch. Rialta Oriflamme O'Solitare (Ch. Geewilliker's de Sang Bleu ex. Ch. Solitaire's Belle Boyd) finished his championship title in five shows with all major wins and has also placed in the Non-Sporting group.

ROBINSON—Active: 1940s. Mr. P. Jones Robinson was a breeder in the 1940s and handled many of the Kelso dogs in the show ring. His foundation bitch was Ch. Riquette of Kelso (Ch. Bromo of Kelso ex Ch. Ricaduena of Kelso). This bitch produced three champions in a litter sired by Maroufke and two more champions in a litter sired by Maroufke's son, Ch. Maquis of Kelso. Another top producer was Ch. Kiska of Kelso, a producer of many champions, including Ch. Alhambra Victory of Kelso, a great Schipperke sire. A litter brother of Kiska, Ch. Hannibal of Kelso, sired several champions.

ROETMOP—Active: 1960s/present. Owner: Marj Kuyt of British Columbia, Canada. The top-winning Schipperke in Canada from 1967 to 1973 was Am/Can Ch. Roetmop Lucifer, Am/Can CD, Can TD. This dog's sire was Ch. Del-Dorel's Stardom. Roetmop kennels has bred many Schipperkes whose names are seen in the pedigrees of many present-day champions.

ROMONT—Active: 1940s/1960s. Owner: Madeline Baiter of New Jersey. Mrs. Baiter served as President of the Schipperke Club of America, Inc., for many years. She campaigned Ch. Kelso's Kookie of Romont extensively, keeping the breed before the public in an area where he was often the only Schipperke entry at shows. Kookie made many worthwhile wins including a Group First.

ROSE GLEN—Active: 1930s/1960s. Owners: Mr. and Mrs. Glen Trissel of California. The Trissels began with stock acquired from Mr. Cranfield and Mrs. Rand, then added Franswold bloodlines. They showed frequently, finishing a number of champions. One, Ch. Rose Glen Little Lady, was the dam of several champions, all bearing the Rose Glen prefix. Ch. Lady Kaydon of Rose Glen (Ch. Rose Glen Clipper ex Ch. Rose Glen Little Racket), owned by Mr. Don Gilbert, brought further laurels to the Trissels by producing several more champions bearing the Rose Glen name. Rose Glen remained comparatively active into the early 1960's, finishing Ch. Lucky of Rose Glen in 1961.

ROSES—Active: 1960s/1970s. Owner: Rose Thurston of Louisiana. Mr. Randy Fugua was also affiliated with and bred champions under the Roses prefix. Mrs. Thurston owner-handled Ch. Jetstar's General Custer to many outstanding wins, including Best in Show and multiple Group Firsts.

SABLESTAR—Active: 1970s/1980s. Owner: Winifred Bartholomew of California. Mrs. Bartholomew showed actively in California during the 1970s and finished several champions, including Ch. Sablestar Ariadne, dam of six champions.

SAN-DIL—Active: 1950s/1970s. Owner: Ruth Dilly. Mrs. Dilly finished some champions and was the breeder of Ch. Ye Ole Lamplighter of San-Dil, CD, a Best in Show winner. Lamplighter went on to become the sire of ten champions. An outstanding bitch of her breeding was Ch. San-Dil's Poppy (Ch. Notoow's Jet Knight ex Petite Princess of San-Dil), the SCA's Top Winning Bitch for 1971, co-owned by the Kornegays (Jetstar) and Ruth Dilly. San-Dil became the foundation bloodlines for a number of kennels in the United States.

SCHNEREGER—Active: 1929/1940s. Owner: Mr. B. Schnereger of California began with Schipperkes in 1929 and showed frequently in the following ten years. Perhaps his best-known dog was Ch. Schnereger's Smoke, a grandson of My Billy Boy. In later years, Mr. Schnereger became known as a veteran Schipperke Obedience trainer, having two of the early Schipperke degree holders on the West Coast. He was also the trainer of Ch. Maroufke's Shadow, CD, owned by Maude Leonard.

SHALAKO—Active: 1980s/present. Owner: Bette Wynn of Alabama. Two outstanding dogs of her breeding have been Ch. Shalako Bear Cat and Ch. Shalako E. L. Fudge, a son of the renowned Ch. Eatchurheartout de Sang Bleu.

SHERIDAN—Active: 1980s/present. Owners: Sherwood and Diane Harris of Georgia. This kennel was formed with the consolidation of Green Lakes and Ben-De when Sherwood and Diane married in 1988. They are active in breeding and showing, and Mr. Harris is licensed to judge Schipperkes.

SKIPALONG—Active: 1960s/present. Owners: Jack and Fran Griggs of Michigan. One of the best-known and active lines today is the Skipalong Schipperkes of Mr. and Mrs. Griggs. Fran Griggs began exhibiting in Conformation and Obedience during the early 1960s. She then moved to the Chicago area in 1965 and increased her breeding and exhibiting activities. Mrs. Griggs showed several Jet-O bitches and completed their championships. These bitches and/or their offspring then produced many champions.

Top producing matrons include Ch. Whodunit of Jet-O, UD, dam of seven champions, and her daughter Ch. Skipalong's Bon Fyr. Bon Fyr is recognized by the SCA as Top Producing dam of champions with nineteen champion get. Another great producer was Ch. Skipalong's Schisma, dam of nine champions.

Her bitch, Ch. Skipalong's Gidget, a Ch. Del-Dorel's Stardom daughter, won Best of Breed at three Specialties and a Group First. She tied for SCA Top Winning Bitch for 1969. Gidget's litter brother, Ch. Skipalong's Gadget, had a number of Group placings, including several Group Firsts. Gadget was the top producing sire of all Non-Sporting dogs in 1972. A Stardom son, Gadget was the sire of thirty-six champions.

Am/Can/Bel Ch. Skipalong's Echo (Ch. Del-Dorel's Stardom ex Ch. Holzum Nibbler of Jet-O), bred by the Griggs and owned by Fran and Richard Wasserman of New Jersey, was the SCA Top Winning Schipperke for 1971 and

Am/Can Ch. Skipalong's Bottom Line, CDX. This dog is an example of the versatility of the Schipperke, going from the Conformation ring to the Obedience ring with ease.

Ch. Skipalong's Tuff E Nuf, multiple Group placer.

1972. Dogs owned or co-owned by the Griggs captured Best of Breed at Schipperke National Specialties in 1972, 1973, 1974, and 1975. The SCA Top Winning Schipperke for 1973, Ch. Elfe Mir's Billie Billy Bi-Ho, was owned by Fran Griggs and Richard Wasserman. Another Best in Show winner, Ch. Elfe-Mir's a Bounc-En Skipper, was co-owned by the Griggs and Sue McFall of Missouri. The Bouncer and Billy were bred by Effie Meyer of Minnesota. Both these winners were sired by Ch. Del-Dorel's Tuffite, a Stardom son.

Other top Skipalong dogs included the following. Ch. Skipalong's Billy

Ch. Skipalong's Gidget, Non-Sporting Group winner and SCA Top Winning Bitch of 1969.
Bergman

Am/Can/Bel Ch. Skipalong's Echo won multiple Group placements during his show career. In addition, "Echo" was the SCA Top Winning Schipperke for 1971 and 1972. *Tauskey*

Bon Howdy Do, owned by Robert Motzer. This dog was the SCA Top Winning Schipperke for 1975, a Best in Show Winner and sire of seventeen champions. Ch. Skipalong's Malagold Luvalot, owned by George Bernhard, was the SCA Top Winning Schipperke of 1976 and 1977, a Best in Show winner and sire of twelve champions. Ch. Skipalong's O' Baby Face, owned by William and Jeanne Suazo was a Best in Show winner. Ch. Skipalong's El Bimbo Jet, also owned by the Suazos, was the SCA Top Winning Schipperke in 1979, 1980, and 1981, and a multiple Best in Show winner. Ch. Skipalong's Drum Major was the sire of at least twenty champions and Ch. Skipalong's When You Say Bud sired at least twenty-three champions. Ch. Skipalong's Charcoal Kid sired fourteen champions, and Ch. Skipalong's HM Wogglebug TE sired at least ten champions.

Mr. and Mrs. Griggs were also active in the Parent Club, were the editors of the SCA Bulletin for many years, and served as SCA historians.

SLY FOX—Active: 1970s/present. Owners: Rhonda and Dick Lee of Montesano, Washington. This kennel was the home of Ch. Beligue's Genai, the dam of champions. Her offspring also produced champions, including, Ch. Sly Fox's E'Lan's Stutz Bear Kat, sire of eleven champions. Ch. Sly Fox Limited Edition, CD, is the sire of eight champion get.

SMITHSTONE—Active: 1942/1950s. Owners: Mr. and Mrs. Willard H. Smith of Pennsylvania. The Smiths became interested in the breed in 1942. Their first Schipperke was Smithstone Margo of Kelso (Ch. Henri Jaspar of Kelso ex Ch. Dina of Kelso), who later made championship. Margo was soon joined by Smithstone Ink Spot of Kelso and Woofson of Kelso, both sired by Maroufke. Woofson readily became a champion, but Ink Spot had to be retired because of an injury. The Smiths started Smithstone Butcher Boy and Smithstone Clovis of Kelso on their way to championships, and both completed titles in the Midwest with other owners. Ch. Hannibal of Kelso, a son of Maroufke bred by P.

Ch. Skipalong's Gidget Basic Black.

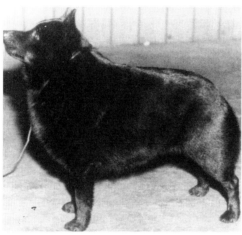

Ch. Skipalong's Malagold Luvalot was the SCA Top Winning Schipperke of 1976 and 1977, a Best in Show winner and sire of twelve champions.

Ch. Skipalong's El Bimbo Jet was a Best in Show winner and was also the winner of multiple Group placements, earning SCA Top Winning Schipperke in 1979, 1980, and 1981, and a multiple Best in Show winner.

Ch. Skipalong's Drum Major, multiple Group placer and sire of twenty champions. *Booth*

Robinson, joined the Smithstone Kennels a little later. From these, the Smiths bred several champions, the most noteworthy being Ch. Smithstone Margette (Ch. Woofson of Kelso ex Ch. Smithstone Margo of Kelso), who won a Group First during World War II when the breed was seldom placing in the Group. She also won Best of Breed at the 1944 specialty show of the Parent breed club and went on to capture second in the Group. Both Ch. Hannibal of Kelso and Ch. Smithstone Margette produced champions.

SORCEROR'S—Active: 1970s/1980s. Owner: Rilda Walton of Texas. Mrs. Walton was a dedicated breeder and bred Sorceror's Maat and Ch. Sorceror's Gladiator. As an owner-handler, she finished Ch. Glen Kay's Emdore, Ch. Paddolin's Bac Talk of A.R.E.S., Ch. Glen Kay's Starbright, Ch. Padolin's Bar Sinister, and others. Active in Obedience, she guided her Schipperkes to many titles in Obedience, including CDX.

SPINDRIFT—Active: 1970s/present. Owners: Richard and Eileen Lane of California. Formerly known as Lenrik, the Lanes began with stock from the Jetstar line. An outstanding dog was Ch. Spindrift Sarahtoga, a multiple Group placer and sire of at least twenty-nine champion offspring. Another of their dogs, Ch. Jetstar's Jaguar of Len-rik, was the sire of twelve champions, including Ch. Eatchurheartout de Sang Bleu, the SCA Top Winning Schipperke for 1982, 1983, 1984, and 1985. Ch. Jetstar's Jaguar of Lenrik and another Spindrift dog, Ch. Spindrift Suede, are the grandsires of Ch. Dream On's One In A Million, the breed's top Best in Show winner and SCA Top Winning Schipperke for 1986, 1987, 1988, 1989, and 1990.

STARBROOK—Active: 1950s/1970s. Owners: Mr. and Mrs. Clarence Westney of Florida. The Westneys were regular exhibitors in the early 1960s in Florida. They finished champions there, then moved to California in 1966,

73

Ch. Skipalong's HM Wogglebug TE, multiple Group placer and sire of ten champions. *Bergman*

completed titles on other dogs, and bred a number of champions owned by other people. Their foundation homebred stud was Ch. Starbrook Sagittarius, the sire of five champions. The foundation bitch, Ch. Lady Haila of Gaybrook, produced six champions in America and a French champion. Her daughter, Ch. Starbrook Savoirfaire, tied for Top Winning Bitch in 1966.

SUNSET—Active: 1970s. Owners: Mr. and Mrs. Charles Walker of Oregon. Some of their winners have been Ch. Sunset's Oh Yoy Yoy and Ch. Sunset's Jim Dandy, both of whom sired champions, Ch. Sunset's Fancy Nancy and Ch. Sunset's Josie Posie. The latter was owned by Elizabeth Catchings of Pennsylvania. This kennel prefix has recently been used by another breeder but has no connection with Mr. Walker's dogs.

TI-DE—Active: 1940s. Owner: Doris Daudelin from New England. From her breeding came Ch. Ti-De Son of Ti, CDX, a Schipperke piloted to his championship and Obedience titles by his owner, Howard Claussen. Ti-De was a half-brother to Mr. Claussen's earlier record-making Ch. Michael Son of Ti, CDX. Mrs. Daudelin Piloted Ch. Black Pepper Son of Ti, CD, to his championship. All three were sired by Titi of Kelso, son of Ch. 'Ti Noir of Kelso.

TI NOIR—Active: 1940s/1950s. Owners: Mr. and Mrs. H. Harshman in California. The Harshmans actively bred and exhibited Schipperkes during the 1940s, showing some to championship, including their first purchase, Sparkey Knight. Ch. Deedeen of Kelso, a Maroufke daughter, gave them two champions bearing the 'Ti Noir prefix. In the 1950s, Ch. Ti Noir Princess Victoria won many Best of Breed wins and Group placings, including two Group Firsts.

TONI—Active: 1950s/1970s. Owners: Mrs. Walter Lake and her daughter, Toni Lake. The Lakes began as Obedience enthusiasts as well as Conformation exhibitors. During the 1950s, they exhibited two champions with Obedience degrees. Of particular note was Ch. Toni's Tinka Tu of Beaumont, UD. Mrs. Lake met with considerable success when she bred to the Ch. Dark Star of Cledlo line, then line-bred on this line. She showed extensively during the 1960s, finishing titles on many Schipperkes.

Ch. Toni's Waltzing Matilda achieved the top producing record for a bitch in this breed, with nineteen champion get. Ch. Toni's Waltzing Shadow, another Lake Schipperke, was SCA Top Winning Schipperke Bitch for 1965. Other top producing bitches were Ch. Toni's Dusty Storm Shadow, dam of six champions, and Ch. Toni's Sunday Star Dust, dam of eight champions. Ch. Toni's Shadow of Dark Star (a Dark Star son) was shown extensively and successfully with numerous Group placings and several Group Firsts. He was the SCA Top Winning Schipperke for 1965, and sired twenty-one champions. Ch. Toni's Duplicator of Dark Star, another Dark Star son, was also campaigned. This dog placed repeatedly in Groups and won at least ten Group Firsts. He climaxed this career with a Best in Show and was the sire of fifteen champions. Ch. Helart's Ragamuffin (another Dark Star son) was a leading winner. Mrs. Lake also bred a large number of Schipperkes that became champions under other ownership, including Best in Show winners Ch. Toni's Mark of Dark Star and Ch. Toni's Little Nemo.

TUDOX—Active: 1970s/present. Owners: Dr. Donald and Shirley Quillen of Ohio. The Quillens began with a Schipperke purchased from the Skipalong kennels of Jack and Fran Griggs. This bitch, Ch. Skipalong's Bounc 'N Button, Am/Can UD, acquired her AKC championship and Utility Dog titles in the United States, and earned a U-UD from the United Kennel Club and a Canadian Obedience Champion (UD) title. She is the dam of three champions, including Ch. Tudox Sara Bellum, UD, Can CDX.

VAKKER DAL—Active: 1950s/present. Owner: Miss D. Copley of North Carolina. Miss Copley finished a number of her Vakker-Dal Schipperkes. Her base stock was from Crest O'Shea, but she later introduced Draco blood.

VALKYRA—Active: 1960s/present. Owner: Mrs. John Schnur of Ohio. Valkyra kennels has bred many champions, including Ch. Valkyra Superfox O'Kleingaul, owned by Kleingaul kennels and the dam of twelve champion offspring. Ch. Frostdale Alexander, a top producing sire, was in residence at her kennels.

VALLE VUE—Active: 1950s/present. Owners: Toni and John Strasburger, of Missouri, then Washington state. Toni Martin had been a Schipperke breeder for several years in the 1950s and was active in both Obedience and Conformation. In the 1960s, she acquired and showed to title Ch. Ye Ole Lamplighter of San-Dil, CD. Following her marriage to John Strasburger, Lamplighter was campaigned to many wins, one being a Best in Show in 1968. Lamplighter was also the SCA Top Winning Schipperke for 1968 and the sire of ten champion offspring.

VELART—Active: 1960s/1970s. Owners: Vella and Arthur Root of, Illinois. Their outstanding Schipperke was Ch. Velart Felix (Ch. Walrose Ebony Captain ex Ch. Carlisle's Kookie) who earned numerous Best of Breed wins and Group placings. Mrs. Root's service to the Schipperke Club of America, Inc., and the breed cannot be measured. A research specialist by profession, she did an extensive study and contributed many articles to the SCA Bulletin. She also authored many works, including *A Schipperke Anthology* and *The Official Book of the Schipperke*.

VON KAY—Active: 1960s/present. Owners: Mr. and Mrs. R. T. Kerchiel. The Von Kay Kennels' first champion and foundation stud was Ch. Von Kay's Rip Lee Regardless. His daughter, Ch. Von Kay's Ebony Imp, won a number of Bests of Breed and Group placings. She also produced several champions. In the later 1960s, the Kerchiels purchased Del-Dorel's Tuffite, a Ch. Del-Dorel's Stardom son. Tuffite has had numerous Best of Breed wins and Group placings, including a Group First. In the 1970s, Ch. Von Kay's Electra of Tuff, became the dam of six champion offspring.

WALROSE—Active: 1940 to 1959. Owners: Mr. and Mrs. Walter H. Chute of Illinois. The Walrose Kennels were established during World War II. The Chutes' first pair of Schipperkes came from Jet-O Kennels and both attained championships. One of these dogs, Ch. Captain Kennedy of Jet-O, CD, earned both his Conformation and Obedience titles in 1941. A notable aspect of this accomplishment was that Mr. Chute trained this dog in his backyard by instructions from a book, without any formal class work.

In 1941, Walrose Kennels purchased Ch. Peta of Kelso. With Peta and another Kelso acquisition, the renowned Walrose line was initiated. Bred to Ch. Maroufke of Kelso, Peta whelped the first Walrose celebrity, Ch. Walrose Maroufkin, who amassed twenty-eight Best of Breed awards and sixteen Group placings, including three Group Firsts, the latter being an extremely rare feat at that time. Not since the show careers of Ch. Burke's Tarzan and Ch. Algene's

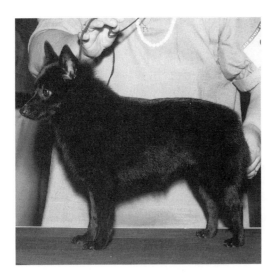

Ch. Valkyra Superfox O'Klein-gaul—dam of twelve champions.
Lidster

76

Chico Para in the 1930s had there been a multiple Group winner in the United States. Maroufkin also made a significant contribution to the breed in the number of champions he sired. Although this kennel remained small in size, Mr. and Mrs. Chute were successful in breeding consecutive winners. The thrilling climax came at the 1949 Westminster K.C. show when Ch. Walrose Maroufkin and his son, Ch. Walrose Black Duke, won Best Brace in Show, a distinguished honor indeed.

The first Walrose star of the 1950s was Ch. Walrose Ebony Captain, a Maroufkin son, who had many wins, including Five Group Firsts. He sired twelve champions, and his name appears in the pedigrees of many of today's champions. Walrose Kennels acquired Dark Star of Cledlo from Mr. and Mrs. Howard Dietrich. Dark Star completed title in 1955 and had an outstanding show career with ten Group Firsts and four Best in Show honors. This record made him the first multiple Best in Show winner in the breed. He was also the SCA Top Winning Schipperke for the years 1956, 1957, and 1958. He sired eighteen champions, many of whom were outstanding winners themselves. Ch. Walrose Stargin produced ten champion get, and Walrose Honey's Belgium Boy produced thirteen champions. Walrose Kennels bred and showed several other champions.

WATLAND—Active: 1910s/1920s. Owner: Frank Addyman. Mr. Addyman, an all-round judge, bred Schips for some years. Reports say Mr. Addyman was a proponent of the English Schipperke. From his kennel came Watland Wiseacre, the sire of the controversial Yperland Peter Simon, which in turn sired the renowned Ch. Reine Claude of Kelso. Watland Wiseacre was an inbred son of Ch. Teddy R and was entirely from direct Belgian bloodlines.

WIL-CLE—Active: 1970s/present. Owner: Wilma Dame of Michigan. Mrs. Dame is an ardent exhibitor in Obedience. She acquired her first Schipperkes from the Noirmont kennels. One of her most outstanding Obedience winners was Wil-Cle Joc Ann de Noirmont, Am/Can UD, (Joc de Noirmont ex Purdy de

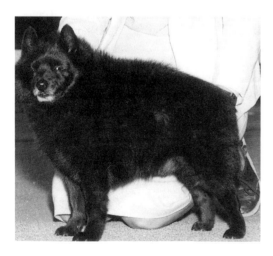

Ch. Von Kay's Belgium Baron of Tuff winning Best of Opposite Sex at the 1985 SCA National Specialty at fourteen years of age.
Seltzer

Noirmont). Called "Kriket," this great little worker was SCA Top Obedience Schipperke for 1971 and again in 1973. She has multiple Highest Scoring Dog in Trial awards to her credit. In addition to her outstanding record in the United States, Kriket has twice been placed in Obedience competition in Canada.

Other Schipperkes owned by Wilma Dame include Wil-Cle Freddy's Free-loader, CDX; Wil-Cle Velvet Pepper, CDX; and Wil-Cle Skipper, CD. Her most recent winner has been Wil-Cle's Bubbles of Dancar (Ch. Skipalong's Upper Case ex Wil-Cle Joc Ann de Noirmont, UD) Following in her mother's footsteps, "Bubbles" also has multiple High in Trial awards. She was the SCA Top Obedience Schipperke in 1980, 1981, 1982, and 1983.

WILSON—Active: 1950s/1970s. Owners: Mr. and Mrs. James Wilson of Missouri. The Wilsons started exhibiting in the mid-1960s. Much of their basic stock came from the Donrho Kennels, and they finished championship title on a large number of Schipperkes. The star of the kennel was Ch. Wilson's Flash Lightning, who won a Best in Show in 1968 in addition to other Best of Breed wins and Group placings. Their great producing matron was Ch. Donrho's Lady Portia who produced eleven champions, while two of their stud dogs, Ch. Donrho's Ebony Buster and Ch. Donrho's Ebony Donel, sired several champions each.

WYM WEY—Active: 1970s. Owner: Gwena Weymouth. One of the best known Schipperkes from her kennel was Ch. Wym Wey Witches Brew, the dam of several champions.

YPERLAND—Active: 1910s/1940s. Owners: Mr. and Mrs. Victor Verhelle of New Jersey. Although Mr. Verhelle was born in Belgium, he did not own any Schipperkes while he lived there. Founded in 1910, Yperland Kennels was the largest Schipperke kennel prior to the mid-1920s. They maintained an average of forty dogs. They imported a number of Schipperkes from Belgium, along with some from England, and combined these bloodlines with their early-American stock. A prolific writer on the breed in the 1920s once described Mr. Verhelle as "The Father of the Breed in America." Certainly, Yperland Kennels produced hundreds of Schipperkes, including champions Ch. Rubio, Am/Can Ch. Seeshes Camelia, and Ch. Fitzi. Yperland Peter Simon was bred and owned by the Yperland Kennels. While Simon finished his title, he was much used as a stud for several years. At the time of the bitter controversy between the proponents of the so-called English and Belgian types, Yperland Peter Simon was the object of a discussion over whether or not he was mainly English in origin. Edward K. Aldrich, Jr., settled the argument by tracing Simon's pedigree back through the stud books and proved that Simon was mostly of Belgian blood. However, it should be remembered that the English Schipperkes originally came from Belgium. It was the selection of breeding stock that differed in the two countries, resulting in the different type developed in England.

When the breed reached a low ebb after World War I, Yperland Kennels kept on with a few dogs and appeared at Westminster when only a few Schipperkes were being shown. This kept the public informed that there was such a breed. On October 15, 1927, a Schipperke first received the coveted Best in Show award in the United States. This honor was won by Yperland Jet Black Skipper (AKC #543212) at the Middlesex County Kennel Club show in Newton, Massachusetts. Skipper was bred by Yperland Kennels and owned by Dr. C. Hammett Rogers of Newport, Rhode Island. His sire was the Belgian import, Black de Veeweyde of Yperland, and his dam was an Yperland Peter Simon daughter. Curiously enough, this dog did not do well at other shows and was retired without attaining championship status.

Two examples of the diplomas awarded to Schipperkes in Belgium prior to World War I (top) and World War II (bottom). The painter Delin set the scene at the marketplace in Brussels. The cobbler is shown cutting off the tail of a Schipperke dog who, according to Belgium legend, trespassed on the neighbor's property while courting the neighbor's bitch.

5

The Twentieth Century: The Schipperke in Other Countries

BELGIUM

AFTER THE AUSPICIOUS BEGINNING of Belgium's Schipperkes Club, entries at shows improved. In 1904, the first Belgian championship certificates (C.A.C.) were awarded. Five Schipperkes were granted this coveted title of merit: Demon de l'Enfer, Exter Ida, Joseph II, Rita de l'Enfer, and Trazegnies. The first Schipperke to compete and earn that title was Ch. Exter Ida in 1905.

The first Belgian Standard divided the size of the breed into two weight classes: large, twenty-pound maximum and small, twelve-pound maximum with no minimum being stated. On July 12, 1904, perhaps to appease various fanciers who favored a diminutive size, a third class weighing less than seven pounds, designated as Toy Schipperkes, was added to the standard. Toy Schipperkes began to be registered as such in the L.O.S.H. beginning with Volume 24 published in 1906.

In the years preceding World War I, Messrs. F. Reusens (Exter) and J. Drossart (de l'Enfer) were the most active breeders. Four of the six champion titles awarded prior to World War I carried the Exter prefix and one the de l'Enfer name. Although breeding suffered a great deal during World War I, the basic bloodlines were preserved for posterity.

During this era, registration in Belgium was conducted differently from that in the United States. A dog was not required to have three generations of registered ancestors and could be registered if it had sufficient quality to win at shows. This provision could have caused a certain amount of carelessness, as many people in Belgium kept purebred dogs for generations without bothering to register them.

The era of the 1920s and 1930s might be called the Golden Age of the Schipperke in Belgium. Show entries were at their peak, and a number of breeders were actively engaged. It was during this active period (1924 to 1939) that numerous Schipperkes were exported to other countries, particularly France, England, and the United States. Many of these exports became the principal foundation of champion bloodlines in those countries.

One of the Schipperkes Club founders and for many years its secretary was Victor Fally, chief veterinarian for the City of Brussels. His kennel name of "de l'Obberg," taken from the street of the same name in Wemmel, was often seen in the pedigrees of Belgian dogs of the 20s. Dr. Fally and his wife were Schipperke judges, and Madame Fally enjoyed the distinction of being the only woman judge of the breed. It was said that Mr. Fally bred for short bodies and a rather short head, preferring the expression with a larger eye and several shades lighter than the small, oval, dark eye described in the Standard. Dr. Fally believed that the modern tendency toward apartment living was making the very small or Toy variety of the breed more desirable and so specialized in producing Toy Schipperkes weighing less than seven pounds. The only known Schipperke exported to the United States from his de l'Obberg Kennel was Ginette de l'Obberg, imported by Mr. C. W. Geier of Pennsylvania and later owned by Mrs. Hogarth of Rhode Island.

An extensive and active breeder in the 1920s was Mr. F. de Coorebyter of Destelbergen. His kennel, Ter Meeren, was named for the Chateau de Ter Meeren, his home. The Ter Meeren stock was descended from the distinguished Exter line, tracing back directly to Franz. It was said that Schipperkes of his breeding tended to be shorter in coat than most other Schipperkes of this era. The Ter Meeren name appears in American pedigrees through Ch. Bebe de Ter Meeren of Kelso, the fountain head of an outstanding champion-producing family in the United States.

Although Emile Schets had bred Schipperkes in the early 1900s, he became best known for his extensive breeding and exhibiting after World War I. He used the kennel name "de Veeweyde" after the street where he and his wife resided in Anderlecht, a town which later became a part of greater Brussels. An article about Schipperkes printed in *Chasse Et Pêche* for August 25, 1934, described Mr. Schets as a worthy successor to Mr. Reusens ("Father of the Schipperke"), asserting that Mr. Schets had been successful in breeding the ideal head by eliminating the too-prominent stop of the past through slow and persevering selection. This was achieved without the snipey muzzle of the over-elongated variety. Champion Poilu (1922), the second Schipperke to attain championship status in Belgium after the end of hostilities, was bred by Mr. Schets and whelped in 1918 during the war. Ch. Poilu's bloodlines later established two of the most important champion-producing male lines in the States. The Veeweyde Kennel was said to be more successful than most in securing a good head with a short body, a combination always difficult to attain in breeding Schipperkes.

The Post War Era

After World War I, show entries again increased until a record number of eighty-one Schipperkes were benched for the club's Specialty show, held April 6, 1930, in Brussels. This was the largest number of Schipperkes ever assembled at one time in Belgium. Entries included Ch. Toto de l'Esperance, then ten years old, Ch. Arsouille de l'Erebe, his son Ch. Da's Gelukt, and Ch. Dolette de Veeweyde who was imported to the United States later that year by Kelso Kennels. Best of Breed was won by Emile Schets's Rico de Veeweyde (later a champion). Rico further added to his laurels by winning the Group at the Specialty show in 1932 under an English judge, a singular honor indeed. Rico later sired a litter which establish Rico's bloodline as a leading champion-producing line in the United States. Mr. Schets retired by 1940 after some sixty-five years of breeding.

The Bois Mures Kennel was owned by Auguste Prevost of Binche. Although this kennel existed only a brief time, it was prominent and made famous by Marouf, a much-used stud in the 1920s. Marouf was dog bred by Mr. Schets and owned by Mr. Prevost. Marouf left his mark on the breed through his five outstanding champion daughters, Belgium Champions Boule des Bois Mures, Alka des Bois Mures, and Dolette de Veeweyde, American Ch. Flore de Veeweyde, Belg., French, and American Ch. Celtic des Bois Mures. Ch. Dolette de Veeweyde, bred by Mr. Schets, twice won the honor of Best Dog in Show in Belgium, including a Best in Show at the eminent Société Royale Saint-Hubert show in 1928. Her daughter, Celtic des Bois Mures accumulated more sensational wins than any other Belgian Schipperke in so short a time. She also won a Best in Show award when only a year old at the Specialty show in Brussels in 1928, defeating the favorite, Ch. Arsouille de l'Erebe. In 1930, Mr. Prevost gave up breeding and sold most of his Schipperkes to other fanciers in France. Only a few dogs were kept for his own pleasure. Celtic was sold to Dr. Alexis before she had secured her Belgian title, but she won her French championship in short order. Ch. Dolette de Veeweyde was exported to the Kelso Kennels in America. Marouf was also exported to the United States but, because he did not have a three-generation certified pedigree, he was denied registration with the American Kennel Club.

Mr. Rene Vander Snickt owned the de l'Esperance Kennel. He was secretary of the Schipperkes Club in 1914. He later served as president upon the death of Mr. Du Pre, until his own death in the mid-1950s. He had two champions in the 1920s, namely, Ch. Pati de Wolver and Ch. Toto de l'Esperance. Toto appears in many older American pedigrees as well as Belgian and French ones. He later acquired Marius des Lutins Noirs, a grandson Ch. Toto de l'Esperance. Marius attained his championship title in 1932 and became the founder of many winning Belgian and French bloodlines. His daughter, Annette de l'Esperance, and a son, Brutus de la Buche, were both exported to the United States in late 1938 by Mr. and Mrs. Rene Isler of Illinois. Another son of Marius, Binchou de la Buche of Schippland, was exported to England. Dogs of his bloodline later were exported to the Union of South Africa. Therefore, it can be said that Ch. Marius des Lutins Noirs has had an important influence on the breed worldwide.

Another illustrious Belgian Schipperke, Ch. Dina owned by Mr. A. Dekeyser of France, added fame to the breed in 1930 by winning Best in Show honors at all-breed shows in Lille and Paris, France. Dina was bred in Belgium and attained her title there in 1931. She lacked a three-generation pedigree and was thus prevented from being exported to the United States.

In 1930, the King of Belgium granted the title of Royal Schipperkes Club to the original Belgian breed club. This title is granted when a club has been in existence for twenty-five years. In that year the Schipperkes Club had been in active existence for forty-two years and was well deserving of this distinction.

The mid-1930s saw the rise of an important kennel, the de Royghem kennel owned by Mr. Florimond Verbanck of Ghent, destined to become the leading Schipperke kennel in Belgium. Mr. Verbanck began his breeding activities mainly with Gentbrugge, Ter Meeren, Veeweyde, and l'Esperance bloodlines and bred more Belgium champions than any other breeder throughout the Schipperke's history in Belgium for that era.

World War II

World War II had a devastating effect on Schipperkes. Many breeders abandoned their activities and, during the years of occupation, several older breeders died, including Mr. Fally and Mr. Schets. When communications were reopened, Mr. R. Vander Snickt wrote that he was the only survivor among the older breeders. His Ch. Eastern Hope Freddy made title in 1941 during the early part of the war and was the only Belgian champion still living when peace came. Other Schipperkes survived after the hostilities ended but, unfortunately, few new breeders emerged to take the place of those lost during the war years. As shows reopened in the late 1940s, Mr. Florimond Verbanck became the primary and often the only, exhibitor. His first homebred champion, Ch. Jupiter de Royghem, died during the war but Mr. Verbanck campaigned a number of Schipperkes to their championships beginning with Ch. Type de Royghem in 1947.

FRANCE

France and Belgium share a common boundary, and the populations of the two countries have mixed for centuries although little is known about the Schipperke in France before 1919. In 1920, in Angevin, Ernest Robert began to breed Schipperkes for conformation. He used the kennel name "des Lutins Noirs," which means "the black imps." The basis of his kennel was Champion Tac, the forerunner of many of the best Schipperkes on the Continent. Subsequently, Mr. Robert continued to import excellent specimens from Belgium, permitting him to maintain quality breeding. In 1924, one of his neighbors, Mr. Arin (de Ker Mano, mainly a breeder of sheepherding dogs) was entranced by the Schipperke and began to breed them. Others soon followed, and in the days just after the first World War Mr. Dekeyser of the des Fortifs kennel, Lille, and Beaulieu sur Layon, Main et Loire, became serious breeders and owners. Schipperkes attaining the greatest distinction in France after World War I were Ch. Tac, Ch. Tiky du M'nu Bos, Ch. Musky de l'Enfer, Ch. Tip de Ker Mano, Ch. Ella de Ker Mano, Ch. Eva de Ker Mano, Ch. Dolette de Valencay, Ch. Gaby de Ker Mano, Sanior Coquin, Ch. Iris des Rolls, Ch. Java des Fortifs, and Dina, who could not attain her championship as her origin was not known.

During the 1930s Ch. Marius des Lutins Noirs, a descendant of Ch. Tac, was unquestionably the best male in the country. The breed increased somewhat in popularity; however, at the outbreak of war there were still just half-a-dozen established breeders. When hostilities ceased in 1945, three bitches had survived; two with Mr. Robert and one with Mr. George Arin. Only Mr. Robert began breeding again, importing essential revitalizing stock from Belgium. Two notable new breeders now came on the scene, both of whom were to contribute significantly to the furthering of the breed; Mme. Lebrocqui of the duVal des Roses kennel, near Paris, and Mr. Schamps of the de la Mottelette kennel in the north. Mr. Schamps acquired several good breeding dogs when de Royghem was dissolved. As his breeding success increased, he improved his stock and imported several more Schipperkes from Belgium, as well as Oliver II of Kelso from America.

Around 1950 Mrs. Hevin (de Bord des Etangs) gave an important boost to the French breeding by importing several American Schipperkes from Miss Ormiston (Kelso) and a Belgian Schipperke from Fl. Verbanck (de Royghem). Unfortunately, Mrs. Hevin ceased breeding when she ended her residence in the countryside.

Mr. Robert helped found the Schipperkes Club of France in 1928. Dr. Bourdais (de Pen Luhern) served as its first president until 1929, when Dr. Alexis (de Valencay) succeeded him. Mr. E. Robert, the aged doyen, assumed the presidency of the Schipperkes Club of France after the death of Dr. Alexis, and held this post until his own death in 1973.

The ruling body in France is the Federation Cynologigue International

(FCI). Dog shows are recognized by the Société Centrale Canine, the SCC, or the French Kennel Club, which operates under the wing of the Ministry of Agriculture. There are also several shows organized by unregistered societies, but these tend to focus on sporting interests. There are no Obedience classes for Group IX dogs, which includes Schipperkes.

The Belgian Schipperke Standard is worded so that only black dogs may be exhibited at shows. To become a national champion, a Schipperke must win three or four CCs, depending on the importance of each show, and must include a win at the prestigious Paris shows or at a show restricted to the breed. The title of International Champion is acquired by winning four CCs in three different countries belonging to the FCI over a period of at least a year. Breeders work hard to keep the Schipperke name in front of the public eye, and slow but steady progress is being made in the breed.

ENGLAND

The Northern Schipperke Club of England was founded in March, 1905, and within a few years the club was holding a well-attended annual meeting. This club adopted the breed Standard approved by the original Schipperke Club of England in the 1800s, bringing the number of active clubs in England to three. All of these clubs remained active for a number of years.

One of England's current winning Schipperkes is Ch. Aradet Cannon Ball Express. This Schipperke has won 14 Best in Show awards, including 11 at Open shows and 3 National Specialty wins. He was also Best of Breed at Crufts in 1983 and 1984.   *Pearce*

The names of English-bred Schipperkes appear in some extended American pedigrees through Ch. Joy of Greta (born June 1901, Champion in 1903), bred by Mr. G. Collin, and through Mr. Dean-Willis's Ch. Bapton Fox, born June 1903, Champion 1906. The A. J. Yates "Don" prefix is also to be found in some American pedigrees. Mr. and Mrs. T. Shepherd founded Royd Kennels in 1910. Their best-known dog, Ch. Royd Oregonian, was whelped June 5, 1914, and attained his championship in 1920. The Royds later became well-known judges but continued to breed Schipperkes. The O'the North Kennels of Mr. and Mrs. E. B. Holmes also opened in 1910 with the purchase of Paul Pry. They bred and owned many outstanding Schipperkes, including Bette O'the North, who was exported to America, and Ch. Dan O'the North, a tenth-generation breeding from their original Schipperke Paul Pry.

After World War I, in February of 1920, the Northern Schipperke Club amended the original breed Standard to allow solid colored non-black coats which were "self colored and harsh. Noses and tails black and the eyes dark." In the decade after the Standard was altered, the original Schipperke Club and the St. Hubert Schipperke Club, both of which opposed non-black Schipperkes, terminated their existance.

Bramber Kennels was owned by Olive MacCarthy. She began in 1929 with Tinker Top. In later years, she bred Ch. Black Speck of Bramber, Ch. June Girl, and Ch. Rising Light of Bramber. The latter two were exported to South Africa. Miss MacCarthy also exported Schipperkes to California, Brazil, and Sweden.

The Ludfords of Schippland fame imported Binchou de la Buche from Belgium in 1939. Ch. Gnome of Schippland, born December 1, 1944, was their first champion.

The Sebring Kennels of Mr. and Mrs. R. Smith were well known. Monty of Sebring and Jessica of Sebring went to Kelso Kennels. Monty had already won two championship certificates here and became an American champion while in Isabel Ormiston's Kelso kennel. Mr. and Mrs. Smith bred the first post-war champion, Joy of Sebring, as well as another beautiful dog, Ch. Nicholas of Sebring.

Mr. Wilton's Blackroot Kennels started in 1951 with Ch. Oakenall Velocette. This Schipperke had already won five certificates under his first owner, who had died. With his new owner, he gained his thirteenth certificate and was Best of Breed many times.

Schipperkes in England weathered severe setbacks in the twentieth century. The first occurred when British authorities placed a ban on breeding and exhibiting during World War I. The [English] Kennel Club withdrew this ban and the war ended, but then rabies broke out in many parts of the country. For over one year, no shows were held and all dogs had to be muzzled.

The second World War was more devastating than the first. This was a time of strict rationing, air raids, bombings, and destruction. A beautiful bitch, Ch. Biddy Imp, died in her owner's arms during an air raid, apparently from a heart attack. Another outstanding dog, Ch. Nil Desperandum, bred and owned

CAC, CACIB, Ch. Kleingaul's Maid in America, imported to Germany. This little Schipperke was Deutsche Bundessiegerin at the prestigious Seiger show in Europe. *Pes*

by Mr. T. Heward, was killed in an air raid while still in his prime. Things were extremely difficult for dog owners, especially as food rationing went on for several years, even after the war ended in 1945. But breeders persevered and eventually the breed began to rebuild.

Championships in England are granted according to the number of puppies registered each year. The Kennel Club keeps track of the number of registrations and then determines the number of championship certificates available for a championship. Certificates are granted only at special championship shows to one dog and one bitch of each breed. All of the certificates must be awarded by separate judges. Champions still compete against non-champions after they have earned their title, thus making it more difficult for other dogs to win.

One of England's current winning Schipperkes is Aradet Cannon Ball Express. This Schipperke has won fourteen Best in Show awards, including eleven at open shows and three National Specialty wins. He was also Best of Breed at Crufts in 1983 and 1984.

FINLAND

Saimi Karkkainen of the Suojan kennel introduced the first Schipperke into Finland in 1964 with the purchase of Sussi, a bitch puppy, from Inga Johansson of

Sweden. Sussi's bloodlines were essentially English, with Mottram, Skipsgreen, Bramber, and Schippland occurring in her pedigree. She finished her Finnish championship and bore six litters, the first of which was sired by Swedish International and Nord Champion Ricky. In 1967 Mrs. Karkkainen imported a dog named Rob Roy from Mrs. Perry's Mascallsbury kennels. Rob Roy did well in Finland, becoming an International and Nord champion. Mrs. Karkkainen then added Arbourland's Seymour to her kennel in 1969, followed by Mascallsbury Lawrence in 1971 and Hallbower Bright Spark in 1972. All became champions in Finland. In 1980 Mrs. Karkkainen had fifteen Schipperkes in her kennel, including Sussi, who was then sixteen years old.

Carita Weigola, of Mandel's kennels, has been a strong influence on the breed in Finland. Her first Schipperke, a bitch named Suojan Bitzie, became a Swedish champion. Bitzie's pedigree includes such English kennel names as Blackroot, Basrah, Mottram, and Mascallsbury. Another of Mrs. Weijola Schipperkes, Jimmy, was imported from Gunborg Eriksson of Sweden. This dog earned the title of Obedience Champion in 1977 at 3½ years of age, making him the only Schipperke in Scandinavia with such a title prior to 1980.

Pipon kennel belongs to Elisabeth Snickars. In 1980, she owned four Schipperkes, including Zwarte Piet van de Holzhoeve, an import from H. J. Hemink of Holland.

Besides small local shows, there are two types of high status shows. They are "National Shows," where Challenge Certificates are awarded, and "International Shows," where CCs and CACIBs (Le Certificate d'aptitude au Championnat International de Beaute) are won. A dog is required to win three CCs to become a Finnish Champion, and one additional CC in Sweden or Norway to earn a championship in those counties. If the dog wins titles from all three countries, it is recognized as a Scandinavian Champion, or Nord Ch. To become an International Champion (Int. Ch.) two CACIBs must be obtained in the country where the dog permanently resides, plus at least one CACIB from each of the other two countries. Int. & Nord Ch. are the most sought-after titles, but quarantine regulations restrict Scandinavian dogs to Scandinavia.

There are ten to fifteen International Shows a year and twenty to thirty National Shows. The two most important International shows are organized by the Finnish Kennel Club and are held in March and November of each year. The Best of Breed winner at the March show is given the title of "Winner of the Year." This is the highest award available. The Schipperke is in the Toy Group and black is the only acceptable color in Finland.

Schipperke owners are spread throughout the whole country and the breed has attained a solid base there with several active and enthusiastic breeders. The rise of the Schipperke's popularity in Finland is indicated by the increase in registrations. In 1964, Sussi was the sole registration; by 1970, the number had risen to twenty-four; and the following year it nearly doubled. The Schipperke Club was formed in 1979 and has more than fifty members.

HOLLAND

The Schipperke appeared in Holland in the past quarter century. During most of this time, the breed was annexed with the Netherlands Keeshond Club.

Many Schipperkes were imported from England and include Oakenall Vosco, brought to Holland by Mr. de Groot in the early 1950s; Aerokens Admiral and Aerokens Ginette, purchased by Mr. E. C. Thomas in the 1970s; and Gamble of Schippland, imported by Mrs. R. Harmsen-Rispens in 1972.

Mr. Cor van Rodijnen, Van Sanquinicus kennel, imported several Belgian Schipperkes before attending Crufts in 1969. He purchased and imported a Schipperke male, Hallbower Magnus. Magnus won eleven CCs and founded the bloodlines of some of the best Schipperkes living in Holland.

One of the best dogs in recent years was Champion and International Champion Alex Happy van Sanquinicus, owned by Mrs. R. Harmsen-Rispens. This dog became a World Champion in 1977. The title of World Champion is awarded at a show called the "Seiger." The Seiger show is held in a different country each time, and only champions are allowed to compete. Dogs may come from any country, although Britain is excluded because of the quarantine laws.

Mr. Cor van Rodijnen imported a colored Schipperke dog, Sylvadown Crocus Boy, in 1974. In Holland, however, black is the only recognized color for a Schipperke, and colored Schipperkes are strictly forbidden in the show ring. A debate regarding the admission of colored Schipperkes ensued. A small, fairly influential group wished to promote the English Standard, while the majority wished to continue with the long-established FCI Standard. The Schipperke Club van Nederland was formed with the colored Schipperke breeders Mr. Langout and Mr. C. van Rodijnen the most prominent members. Breeders wishing to keep the Schipperke black banded together and published a review entitled "Friends of the Schipperke" promoting the Belgian Standard. Despite the debate, the breed's popularity is growing and should continue to grow in the future.

NEW ZEALAND

There have been three distinct and separate phases of Schipperke breeding in New Zealand in the twentieth century. Between each phase the breed apparently died out or at least weakened to the extent that there was no significant breeding or showing.

Evidence of the first Schipperke imports was discovered in the archives of the Canterbury Public Library. Large bound volumes of newspapers, published since the 1850s, were stored for reference. On August 7, 1907, the *Weekly Press* published an article entitled "Some Costly Toy Dogs," which stated: "Dr. Hammersley of Christchurch has recently imported some Schipperkes and Toy Pomeranians. The Schipperkes are the first ever imported into New Zealand." The report went on to relate that the four English dogs had cost Dr. Hammersley

Ch. Black Power of Jet-O became one of Australia's foundation sires. His son was the first Schipperke in Australia to win Best in Show. His granddaughter made history by winning Best Junior in Group at the New Zealand National Dog Show in 1980.   *Storey*

over 200 pounds on release from quarantine—quite a significant sum in those days. Photos of the dogs appeared with the article.

Dr. Hammersley was a surgeon who worked at Christchurch Public Hospital and lived in a large house in Christchurch. He was a man of means with several servants and his own carriage and horses to transport him around the city. His dogs were mostly accommodated in individual kennels at the rear of his property. His niece described the kennels as little houses with doors, windows, and pitched roofs. As a very young girl she remembered going to visit her uncle to see his dogs.

After 1916 there are no known records of Schipperkes being shown or bred, and they disappeared from the scene.

The next phase began in August of 1926 with the arrival of Mr. and Mrs. Marshall from England. When they visited New Zealand in 1921, Mrs. Marshall was already active in Schipperkes in the United Kingdom. They found New Zealand to their liking and returned to settle at Mangere, near Auckland, with their dogs. The New Zealand Kennel Club files attest to the registration of their three Schipperkes: Kilmaronock Chum, Kilmaronock Teckla, and Kilmaronock Delme. After their arrival, Mr. Marshall embarked on a series of antics which ensured he would became a legend in New Zealand Kennel Club history. In the book *Dogsbody—The Story of the New Zealand Kennel Club*, by Stewart Lusk, an entire chapter is devoted to ''Robert Marshall and The Great Rebellion.'' In 1932, as a result of his misdemeanors, Mr. Marshall was banned from New Zealand Kennel Club. Mr. Marshall continued to breed Schipperkes and imported a Schipperke stud dog, Royd Rangi, in 1937. Because Mr. Marshall was banned, all litters bred by the Marshalls in 1941, 1946, and 1947 could not be registered.

Finally, in 1949, Mr. Marshall requested that the suspension on his family dogs be lifted. The executive council agreed to allow them to be reinstated, but required the Marshalls to sign a statutory declaration that they would conform with New Zealand Kennel Club regulations before the Kennel Club would reinstate them. Laurie Castle lived in Auckland and had one of Mr. Marshall's Schipperkes. She was photographed about 1936 holding this Schipperke, named Mabs, in her arms. Tragically, in 1943 at the age of 13 years this bitch was savaged by a large dog and had to be destroyed. Mr. and Mrs. Marshall imported another Schipperke from England in 1950, Ylminster Rebel, bred by Mrs. R. Davey. After this, their efforts in the breed ceased and Schipperkes apparently became extinct in New Zealand for the second time.

In 1968, interest in the breed was revived again when, independent of each other, two dog fanciers became interested in the breed. Mavis Lightfoot, from Auckland, was well known for her Longbay Dachshunds and Italian Greyhounds. She journeyed to Australia and became acquainted with the Sunnyslopes Schipperkes, owned by Amy Cunich. Robert and Gloria Thompson, of Christchurch, successfully bred Pembroke Welsh Corgis under their Weymouth suffix. They, too, desired a second breed. Robert Thompson wrote to Amy Cunich seeking breeding stock. On November 1, 1968, two Schipperkes arrived in the same crate on an aircraft from Sydney. A bitch, Sunnyslopes Lady Gay, was for Mavis Lightfoot, and a dog, Warrenville Dixie's Lad, was Robert Thompson's.

The following year Mrs. Lightfoot returned to Australia with several dogs for a showing holiday. Lady Gay came into season during this trip and was bred to Australian Ch. Sunnyslopes Starturnand. She had a litter of three puppies after her return to Auckland. Mrs. Lightfoot also sent down Lady Gay to be bred to Dixie in 1970, and, again, she produced three puppies. Mrs. Lightfoot never bred any more Schipperkes after the second litter.

Mr. Thompson imported three Schipperke bitches from Australia between 1968 and 1970. Each of these females was bred to his dog Dixie. From the first litter (Warrenville Dixie's Lad ex Gunyah Needles), Robert Thompson sold a bitch puppy to Donald Kitto of Timaru, beginning Mr. Kitto's association with the breed that continues to the present. Under his Westgarth prefix Mr. Kitto has successfully bred winners in both the conformation and obedience rings. He was the first person in New Zealand to own a Schipperke Obedience Champion, when his dog became Ch. & Ob. Ch. Westgarth Jathro Rono, CDX.

From the Thompsons' second litter in 1970 (Warrenville Dixie's Lad ex. Gunyah Royal Inkspot), a bitch puppy named Dinky of Weymouth was sold to Vivienne Fears and her husband Bernard. Mrs. Fears bought four more Schipperkes from the Thompsons, including Gunyah Needles. These were the foundation stock for Exmoor, which became the largest Schipperke kennel in Australia.

No official Schipperke Club exists in New Zealand; however, there is a strong sense of camaraderie among Schipperke folk, and each year a meeting is held among the fanciers attending the National Show. In 1976, these fanciers decided to begin a newsletter, and the quarterly publication "Schipperke News" was initiated. It is mailed to Schipperke owners and fanciers in Australia. The dedication and enthusiasm of breeders today will ensure its continuity and wider acceptance in this country.

SOUTH AFRICA

A popular belief among Schipperke fanciers is that the first Schipperkes to set foot on South African soil were a pair imported by President Steyn of the Orange Free State before the Anglo-Boer war. Although this is a charming tale, there is no documented evidence of Schipperkes in South Africa until Mr. and Mrs. E. T. Capon of Riverton, near Kimberly, imported Pete O'the North from England in 1927. After this dog's introduction, the Capons imported eight other Schipperkes from England in a short period of time, including Ch. Monte O'the North.

During the 1930s, little is known about the breed in this country. After the end of World War II, however, Schipperkes became popular and could be found all over the country. A Schipperke named Royd Rae was imported from England by Mrs. C. E. Priestman in the early 1950s. The Moore family purchased Reeve of Oldway from the English kennel of Mrs. Langton in 1960. Ch. Monte O'the North, Ch. Royd Rae, and Ch. Moorehaven Reeve of Oldway became the foundation stock for the current South African bloodlines. Between them, they have sired numerous winners.

There are approximately fifty general championship shows in South Africa (including Zimbabwe), which are under the control of the Kennel Union of Southern Africa. Schipperkes have placed Best in Show at all-breed Championship Shows and have been awarded numerous placings in the Group rings. Schipperkes have performed well in Obedience competition, and the country boasts Obedience champions as well as conformation champions.

Show judges from many parts of the world have commented favorably on the high standard of the Schipperkes they have judged in South Africa. South African-bred Schipperkes have been exported to Great Britain, the United States of America, Switzerland, Italy, Lebanon, Israel, Bermuda, Kenya, Zambia, and Zimbabwe. The breed is supported by an active club formed in 1959. The club membership published a quarterly bulletin and has a sizable membership.

CANADA

Canada's early Schipperke bloodlines relied on significant contributions by English-bred stock. The first Schipperke registered with the Canadian Kennel Club in 1908 was Siestue Lass, bred by J. and D. Cochran of Hamilton, Ontario, whelped in April 1904. Her sire, El Allwyn, and dam, Lady Somerville, were both claimed to be English stock.

Canadian Ch. Skipakey's Burglar Bob, a Best in Show winning Schipperke in Canada.

In 1908, William Parker purchased and exhibited an English-bred Schipperke at a show in Vancouver, British Columbia. Four years later, Mr. J. C. Smith of Calgary, Alberta, imported a Schipperke from England. He later acquired others, began a breeding program, and exhibited Schipperkes at shows from Calgary, Alberta, to Winnipeg, Manitoba.

Robert Fairclough of Fernie, British Columbia, and Clare Lamplugh and Mr. William Lea, both of Vancouver, British Columbia, imported dogs from England in 1913. In May of 1927, Ellen Brown of Toronto, Ontario, hired an authorized agent, and imported three Schipperkes; one male, Roff O'the North, and two bitches, Mirth O'the North, and Mystery of Winder. Roff O'the North and Mirth O'the North were later shown to their Canadian Championships. She assumed "O'the North," the prefix of Mr. and Mrs. E. B. Holmes of Derby, one of the most prestigious kennel names in England. Both bitches were in whelp before leaving England, but Mystery lost her litter en route. "Mirth," who had been bred to to English Champion Jock O'the North, produced two dogs and two bitches in July of 1929. One dog died, but the three surviving puppies, plus the other imports, formed the foundation stock of the Canadian "O'the North" Kennels. In all, during the next thirty years, Ellen Brown bred more than fifty champions and kept the breed before the public eye in Canada and in the United States.

A number of Schipperkes of Canadian bloodlines can trace their roots back to the 1927 imports, including the Northern Echoes kennels of Alma King; Roetmop kennels, owned by Marjorie Kuyt; and Fairlaur kennels, owned by Fran Hoye. A number of other breeders derive stock from these later three kennels.

Because of Canada's close proximity to the United States, American blood-

Am/Can Ch. Knighttime Banner O'Camplaren was a multiple Best in Show winner in Canada and a Group winner in America.

Paw prints, Inc.

Am/Can Ch. Camplaren's Native Son was Canada's Top Schipperke in 1980, 1981, 1982, and 1983. A Best in Show winner in both America and Canada, he competed four times in Canada's prestigious "Show of Shows," which is open only to Best in Show winners, and won the Group twice. He was ranked second Non-Sporting dog in Canada in 1980.   *Brown*

lines have influenced the type of Schipperke being bred and shown in Canada, whereas the English influence on the Schipperke in Canada after World War II has been negligible. There have been a few English imports, but it is a fact that few, if any, English-bred Schipperkes have attained their Canadian Championships during the past quarter century.

Most shows in Canada take place back-to-back; i.e., two dog clubs organize shows very close together at virtually the same time. Two sets of points are available, a necessary concession to exhibitors who have to travel long distances. Entries of Schipperkes at Canadian shows are not large, but quality appears consistently good as Schipperkes frequently place in the Non-Sporting Group at the larger shows.

The Schipperke Club of Canada was founded in 1965. The Club issues a Newsletter, organizes Booster Shows, and occasionally manages a Specialty Show exclusive to the breed.

6

The Schipperke
Hall of Fame

THE HALL OF FAME honors Schipperkes whose distinquished careers have left a permanent mark on the breed. To be eligible for consideration for the Hall of Fame, the Schipperke must be a combination of one or more of the following: 1) an American-bred dog or bitch who has earned at least one all-breed Best in Show 2) an American-bred Schipperke dog who has sired twenty-five or more American or Canadian champion progeny, 3) an American-bred Schipperke bitch who is the dam of twelve or more American or Canadian champion progeny or 4) an American-bred Schipperke who has earned an all-breed High in Trial, or 5) an American-bred Schipperke who has attained the title of Obedience Trial Champion.

Each of the Schipperkes presented in the following pages has compiled an outstanding record in conformation, Obedience or as a producer and, in many instances, was considered to be among the "greatest" Schipperkes of the day.

CH. MAROUFKE OF KELSO

Although the peerless Ch. Maroufke of Kelso (Ch. Marouf of Kelso ex Ch. Arlette of Kelso) owned and bred by F. Isabel Ormiston, appeared in the show ring before the 1940s, it was during the war years that his incomparable influence began to be felt upon the breed.

Considered by many breeders and fanciers to be the greatest dog produced by Kelso Kennels, Ch. Maroufke of Kelso was the grandson of Isabel Ormiston's original imported foundation pair, Ch. Max de Veeweyde and Ch. Flore de Veeweyde.

By the time Maroufke was retired, he had won fifty Bests of Breed including one at Morris and Essex Kennel Club over a record entry of forty-nine in 1939, five wins at Specialties and an incomparable five Best of Breed wins at Westminster, in addition to numerous Group placings.

Maroufke left a marked influence on breed type, as shown by his record of thirty-two champion get. Nearly every Schipperke attaining a championship in the United States today can trace roots to Maroufke. Ch. Maroufke of Kelso holds a unique place in the Schipperke Hall of Fame.

CH. DARK STAR OF CLEDLO

The distinguished multiple Best in Show winner, Ch. Dark Star of Cledlo (Ch. Lutin of Kelso ex Ch. Portia of Kelso), bred by Mr. and Mrs. Howard Dietrich and owned by Mr. and Mrs. Walter Chute, was one of the top winning Schipperkes of his day. Dark Star completed his title in 1955 and had an outstanding show career. His record includes multiple Group placements, including 10 Group Firsts with four Best in Show Awards. This made Dark Star the first multiple Best in Show winner in America and the top Schipperke for 1956, 1957, and 1958.

Dark Star is also one of the breed's greatest sires of champions. His eighteen champion offspring include such greats as Ch. Del-Dorel's Stardom, with 94 Group placings, 9 Best in Show Awards, and Top Schipperke for 1960, 1961, 1962, 1963, and 1964; Ch. Toni's Shadow of Dark Star, multiple Group winner and Top Schipperke for 1965; Ch. Toni's' Duplicator of Dark Star, winner of 10 Group Firsts and a Best in Show; and Ch. Toni's Mark of Dark Star, UD, a multiple Group winner and Best in Show winner.

In addition, Dark Star sired numerous Schipperkes who were recognized as top producers, including Ch. Corinda of Cledlo, dam of 6 champions, Ch. Walrose Stargin, sire of 10 champions, Ch. Toni's Shadow of Dark Star, sire of 16 champions, and Ch. Del-Dorel's Stardom, sire of 39 champion get.

CH. DEL-DOREL'S STARDOM

Ch. Del-Dorel's Stardom, (Ch. Dark Star of Cledlo ex Ch. Walrose Black Domino) bred and owned by Mr. and Mrs. Del Lasser, was the top winning Schipperke for 1960, 1961, 1962, 1963 and 1964. Stardom's show record includes 94 Group placings, with 23 Group Firsts and 9 Best in Show awards, a record unequaled by any other Schipperke until Ch. Klinahof's Marouf A Draco, a Stardom son.

Stardom was not only the breed's greatest winner in his time, but was also a great sire with 39 champion get. His distinguished offspring include the following: Ch. Klinahof's Marouf A Draco, multiple Best in Show dog; Ch. Skipalong's Gadget, Group winner and the top producing Non-Sporting sire in 1972; Ch. Skipalong's Gadget, Specialty Best of Breed winner and tied for SCA Top Winning Bitch for 1969; Am/Can/Bel Ch. Skipalong's Echo, the top winning Schipperke for 1971 and 1972; Ch. Del-Dorel's Achates, dam of seven champions, and Ch. Del-Dorel's Tuffite, multiple Group winner.

CH. KLINAHOF'S MAROUF A DRACO

Ch. Klinahof's Marouf A Draco (Ch. Del-Dorel's Stardom ex Ch. Holaday's Petite Amanda) bred by Mr. and Mrs. M. J. Mills and owned by Dean J. D. Jones, became the first Schipperke to win more than 10 all-breed Best in Show awards.

Draco's show record is impressive—more than 250 Best of Breed wins, 131 Group placements including 50 Group Firsts and a total of 12 Best in Show wins, being top winning Schipperke for 1969 and 1970.

Draco was also an outstanding producer, having sired 40 champions and tied for top producing Non-Sporting sire in 1971. Notable offspring include Ch. Frostdale Alexander, himself the sire of 17 champion get and Ch. Lynden's Citation, the sire of 29 champions.

CH. EATCHURHEARTOUT DE SANG BLEU

Ch. Eatchurheartout de Sang Bleu (Ch. Jetstar's Jaguar of Len Rik ex Ch. Belle Noire Nothing Else), bred and owned by Greg and Maureen Garrity, was the top winning Schipperke all systems for 1981, 1982, 1983, 1984, and 1985. He was one of only three Schipperkes since World War II to be top winning Schipperke for five consecutive years. "Jojo" amassed 13 all-breed Best in Show awards, including a Best in Show at the renowned Chicago International, 2 National Specialty Best of Breed wins, 310 Best of Breed wins, including Westminister Kennel Club, 58 Group Firsts, 59 Group Seconds, 48 Group Thirds, and 35 Group Fourths. He became one of the only Schipperkes to win "back to back" Best in Show awards.

JoJo has sired at least twenty champions, including Ch. Dream On's One In A Million, the breed's top Best in Show winner and Ch. Shalako's E. L. Fudge, winner of five Best in Show awards to date. A bitch, Ch. Dream On's Thrill of Victory, is a multiple Group placer in Canada. JoJo was one of five puppies in the first litter from de Sang Bleu kennels. All five puppies became champions.

CH. DREAM ON'S ONE IN A MILLION

Ch. Dream On's One In A Million (Ch. Eatchurheartout de Sang Bleu ex Ch. Dream On's Enchantment), bred and owned by William and Marcia Bailey, finished his championship undefeated at eight months of age and began a show career unequaled in the breed. He is the top Schipperke all-breed Best in Show winner, with fifteen. He won 68 Non-Sporting Group Firsts, 59 Seconds, 38 Thirds, 20 Fourths, and four Specialty Bests of Breed. "Chance" also won Best of Breed twice at the Westminister Kennel Club, and went on to a Group Third in 1988 and a Group Second in 1989. This made Chance the only Schipperke to place higher than Group Third at this show and the only Schipperke to place in the Group a second time. In addition, he was SCA Top Winning Schipperke for 1986, 1987, 1988, 1989 and 1990, making him one of only three Schipperkes to hold that title for five consecutive years since World War II. Chance was retired with Best of Breed at the 1991 Schipperke National over a record breaking entry.

Chance has sired at least ten champions. His most notable offspring include Ch. Dream On's Knockout, a multiple Group placer, and Ch. Nanhall's Million Dollar Baby, also a multiple Group placer.

CH. A.R.E.S. MAAH-VELOUS

Ch. A.R.E.S. Maah-velous (Ch. A.R.E.S. Beauregard O Padolin ex Ch. A.R.E.S. Non-stop of Woodland) was bred and is owned by Ellen Stevens and her daughter, Toni Stevens.

Maah-velous is the only bitch to have won two all-breed Best in Show awards. She is also a multiple Group winner and has numerous Group placements to her credit. This record would be outstanding for any Schipperke, and is particularly noteworthy for a bitch. These achievements make her the top winning Best in Show bitch in breed history.

"Maavy's" sire is Ch. A.R.E.S. Beauregard O Padolin, who is also an all-breed Best in Show winner.

CH. JETSTAR'S DHU POINT

Ch. Jetstar's Dhu Point (Ch. Toni's Duplicator of Dark Star ex Ch. Notoow's Princess Mariette), bred by S. and D. J. Kornegay, has sired an unequaled sixty champions, making him the breed's top producing sire. His notable offspring include the following:

Ch. Jetstar's Dust Moppe—Top Winning Schipperke Bitch for the years 1978 and 1979.

Ch. Jetstar's General Custard—an all-breed Best in Show winner and multiple Group placer.

Ch. Jetstar's Jaguar O Len-rik—sire of the distinguished Best in Show winner Ch. Eatchurheartout de Sang Bleu.

CH. SKIPALONG'S BON FYR

Ch. Skipalong's Bon Fyr (Ch. Del-Dorel's Stardom ex Ch. Whodunit of Jet-O, UD) bred by Jack and V. Frances Griggs, not only compiled a good record in the conformation ring, but is recognized as tied for the title of Top Producing dam of champions, with nineteen champion get to her credit.

Among her most noted offspring are;

Ch. Skipalong's Gadget—multiple Group placer, and the Top Producing sire of all Non-sporting dogs in 1972. A Stardom son, Gadget was the sire of thirty-six champions.

Ch. Skipalong's Gidget—also Ch. Del-Dorel's Stardom daughter, and a litter sister to Ch. Skipalong's Gadget. Gidget won Best of Breed at three Specialties and a Group First. She tied for SCA Top Winning Bitch for 1969.

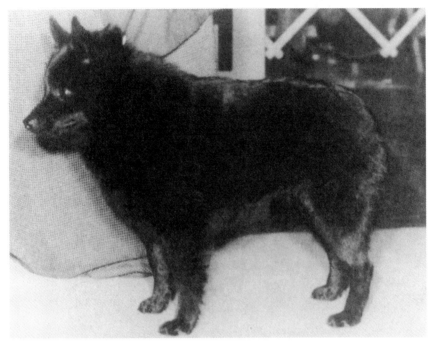

CH. TONI'S WALTZING MATILDA

Ch. Toni's Waltzing Matilda (Ch. Rollingway Black Beauty ex Dun-C's Schatzi) bred and owned by Mrs. Walter Lake, is tied with Ch. Skip-along's Bon Fyr as the breed's top producing dam of champions, with nineteen champion offspring.

Among this bitch champion's most notable offspring are the following;

Ch. Toni's Mark of Dark Star, UD—a son of Ch. Dark Star of Cledlo. Ch. Toni's Mark of Dark Star, UD, was a multiple Group winner and Best in Show winner.

Ch. Toni's Sheba O' Shadow—a multiple Group winner and a producer of champions.

O.T.CH. GRA-BAR'S DANCING DUCHESS

O.T.Ch. Gra-bar's Dancing Duchess, owned and handled by Bobbie Gavin, was the first Obedience Trial Champion Schipperke to be recognized by the American Kennel Club.

Her Obedience career was outstanding, and she earned numerous Highest Scoring Dog in Trial awards, including the very competitive and prestigious 1977 Eastern Regional Division of the Gaines Super Dog competition.

She was the top Obedience Schipperke for the years 1976, 1977, 1978 and 1979 and averaged scores of 196 over the four years of work. She would have undoubtedly achieved many more excellent scores had it not been for the untimely death of her owner.

HOLIDAY, UDT

Holiday, UDT, owned and handled by V. Frances Griggs, earned CD, CDX and UD degrees all within an 8½ month period. She was campaigned extensively and won 87 class Firsts with an amazing 33 Highest Scoring Dog in Trial awards.

Her lifetime show average for the 177 classes in which she participated (with qualifying scores) was 197.5. Holiday had 9 *consecutive* Highest Scoring Dog in Trial and four perfect scores of 200. Holiday has also earned her Tracking Dog title three times. This is an enviable record for anyone in any breed, and one very few may ever equal.

Holiday, UDT was often paired with Gem Jet's Jody, another Griggs Schipperke, who earned a CD degree in 1961, a CDX in 1962 and a UD in 1963 and won many Highest Scoring Dog in Trial awards to form an Obedience brace. This brace received many awards and was noteworthy because Holiday and Jody worked together without a brace lead, they simply worked next to each other, each on her own collar and lead or off-lead side by side.

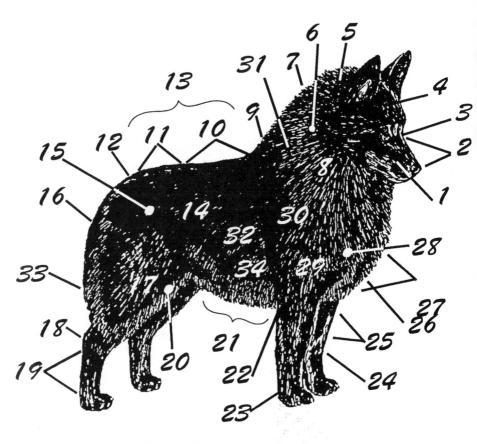

PARTS OF THE SCHIPPERKE

1-Muzzle, 2-Foreface, 3-Stop, 4-Skull, 5-Occiput (center point at the back of the skull), 6-Ruff, 7-Crest of neck, 8-Neck, 9-Withers, 10-Back, 11-Croup, 12-Tail set, 13-Topline, 14-Loin, 15-Point of hip, 16-Point of buttock, 17-Thigh, 18-Hock, 19-Metatarsus, 20-Stifle, 21-Underline, 22-Elbow, 23-Pastern, 24-Knee, 25-Forearm, 26-Jabot, 27-Forechest, 28-Point of shoulder, 29-Upper arm, 30-Shoulder blade, 31-Cape, 32-Ribs, 33-Culotte, 34-Chest

7

Official Standard
of the Schipperke

EACH BREED of dog recognized by the American Kennel Club, Inc., has a Standard of perfection which describes the ideal specimen as envisioned and ratified by each breed's National Specialty club. Thus, the official Standard of the Schipperke describes an ideal Schipperke.

The American Kennel Club does not write breed Standards. This task falls to the breed's National Specialty club. The Schipperke Club of America, Inc., as the Parent specialty club, is charged with this important duty.

The first Standard ratified by the Schipperke Club of America, Inc. was essentially a direct translation of the Belgian Standard. It was later updated and amended in 1935, 1959, and most recently, in 1991. The current Standard is presented here.

GENERAL APPEARANCE

The Schipperke is an agile, active watchdog and hunter of vermin. In appearance he is a small, thickset, cobby, black, tailless dog, with a foxlike face. The dog is square in profile and possesses a distinctive coat, which includes a stand out ruff, cape and culottes. All of these create a unique silhouette, appearing to slope from shoulders to croup. Males are decidedly masculine without coarseness. Bitches are decidedly feminine without overrefinement. Any deviation from the ideal described in the standard should be penalized to the extent of the deviation. Faults common to all breeds are as undesirable in the Schipperke as in any other breed, even though such faults may not be specifically mentioned in the standard.

SIZE, PROPORTION, SUBSTANCE

Size—The suggested height at the highest point of the withers is 11–13 inches for males and 10–12 for bitches. Quality should always take precedence over size. **Proportion**—Square in profile. **Substance**—Thickset.

HEAD

Expression—The expression is questioning, mischievous, impudent, and alert, but never mean or wild. The well proportioned head, accompanied by the correct eyes and ears, will give the dog the proper Schipperke expression.

Skull—The skull is of medium width, narrowing toward the muzzle. Seen in profile with ears laid back, the skull is slightly rounded. The upper jaw is moderately filled in under the eyes, so that, when viewed from above, the head forms a wedge tapering smoothly from the back of the skull to the tip of the nose. The stop is definite but not prominent. The length of the muzzle is slightly less than the length of the skull. **Eyes**—The ideal eyes are small, oval rather than round, dark brown, and placed forward on the head. **Ears**— The ears are small, triangular, placed high on the head, when at attention, very erect. A drop ear or ears is a disqualification. **Nose**—The nose is small and black. **Bite**—The bite must be scissors or level. Any deviation is to be severely penalized.

NECK, TOPLINE, BODY

Neck—The neck is of moderate length, slightly arched, and in balance with the rest of the dog to give correct silhouette. **Topline**—The topline is level or sloping slightly from the withers to the croup. The stand-out ruff adds to the slope, making the dog seem slightly higher at the shoulders than at the rump. **Body**—The chest is broad and deep, and reaches to the elbows. The well sprung ribs (modified oval) are wide behind the shoulders between the front legs. The loin is short, muscular, and moderately drawn up. The croup is broad and well-rounded with the tail docked. No tail is visually discernible.

FOREQUARTERS

The shoulders are well laid back, with the legs extending straight down from the body when viewed from the front. From the side, legs are placed well under the body. Pasterns are short, thick, and strong, but still flexible, showing a slight angle when viewed from the side. Dewclaws are generally removed. Feet are small, round, and tight. Nails are short, strong, and black.

HINDQUARTERS

The hindquarters appear slightly lighter than the forequarters, but are well muscled, and in balance with the front. The hocks are well let down and the stifles are well bent. Extreme angulation is to be penalized. From the rear, the legs extend straight down from the hip through the hock to the feet. Dewclaws must be removed.

COAT

Pattern—The adult coat is highly characteristic and must include several distinct lengths growing naturally in a specific pattern. The coat is short on the face, ears, front of the forelegs and on the hocks; it is medium length on the body, and longer in the ruff, cape, jabot, and culottes. The ruff begins in back of the ears and extends completely around the neck; the cape forms an additional distinct layer extending beyond the ruff; the jabot extends across the chest and down between the front legs. The hair down the middle of the back, starting just behind the cape and continuing over the rump, lies flat. It is slightly shorter than the cape but longer than the hair on the sides of the body and sides of the legs. The coat on the rear of the thighs forms culottes, which should be as long as the ruff. Lack of differentiation in coat lengths should be heavily penalized, as it is an essential breed characteristic.

Texture—The coat is abundant, straight and slightly harsh to the touch. The softer undercoat is dense and short on the body and is very dense around the neck, making the ruff stand out. Silky coats, body coats over three inches in length, or very harsh coats are equally incorrect. **Trimming**—As the Schipperke is a natural breed, only trimming of the whiskers and the hair between the pads of the feet is optional. Any other trimming must not be done.

COLOR

The outercoat must be black. Any color other than a natural black is a disqualification. The undercoat, however, may be slightly lighter. During the shedding period, the coat may take on a transitory reddish cast, which is to be penalized to the degree that it detracts from the overall black appearance of the dog. Graying due to age (seven years or older) or occasional white hairs should not be penalized.

GAIT

Proper Schipperke movement is a smooth, well coordinated, and graceful trot (basically double tracking at a moderate speed), with a tendency to converge gradually toward the center of balance beneath the dog as speed increases. Front and rear must be in perfect balance with good reach in front and drive in the rear. The topline remains level or slightly sloping downward from the shoulders to the rump. Viewed from the front, the elbows remain close to the body. The legs form a straight line from the shoulders through the elbows to the toes, with the feet pointing straight ahead. From the rear, the legs form a straight line from the hip through the hocks to the pads, with the feet pointing straight ahead.

TEMPERAMENT

The Schipperke is curious, interested in everything around him, and is an excellent and faithful little watchdog. He is reserved with strangers and ready to protect his family and property if necessary. He displays a confident and independent personality, reflecting the breed's original purpose as a watchdog and hunter of vermin.

DISQUALIFICATIONS

A drop ear or ears.
Any color other than a natural black.

Approved November 13, 1990
Effective January 1, 1991

8

The Ideal Schipperke

ONE OF THE QUESTIONS commonly asked by the new fancier is, "What does the ideal Schipperke look like?" Although the AKC Standard for the breed describes the Schipperke and may be an adequate guide for experienced breeders and judges, it may not be a satisfactory answer for someone who has not acquired sufficient knowledge of canine structure and breed type to be able to interpret the Standard correctly.

The distinguishing features of Schipperkes are a distinctive silhouette with a distinct ruff and culotte. In appearance, the Schipperke is thickset and cobby— a small black dog possessing plenty of coat, an outstanding ruff and culotte, a "foxy" head with an expressive face, and the complete lack of a tail. The front portion of the dog appears slightly heavier in bone than the rear, but the overall bone structure is relatively fine. All these combine to form a silhouette which does not resemble any other breed.

This characteristic silhouette may be visualized from the outline drawn by Georges Arin, Secretary of the Schipperkes Club de France, and presented here in *Figure 1*. This sketch originally appeared in *Les Echos D'Elevage* in France in 1931 and was later presented by F. Isabel Ormiston in the breed column of the March 1932 *American Kennel Gazette* and caused much controversy among American fanciers. The diagram depicts the correct proportions for a twelve-pound Schipperke. The measurements were obtained by averaging the measurements of six living Belgian and French champions chosen by the French club. The six dogs varied "hardly at all in any measurement, so that the average might be that of any one of the dogs, so similar were they all."

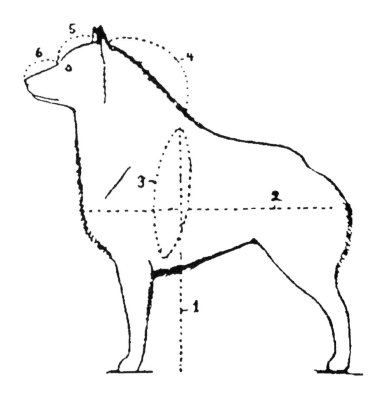

1. 12.36 inches   2. 13.8o inches   3. !7.76 inches
4. 5.43 inches   5. 5.30 inches   6. 2.52 inches

This outline drawn by Mons. Georges Arin, Secretary of the Schipperkes Club de France, originally appeared in *Les Échos D'Élevage* in France in 1931.

The diagram includes the coat, which is an essential part of the Schipperke silhouette, and shows the distinguishing characteristics of the breed at a glance: short, cobby body filling a square, back level or slightly sloping downward from the front to the hindquarters, correct head proportions with small ears. It must be taken as only *representing* the ideal because it does contain a slight amount of exaggeration in order to emphasize certain important traits. One fault is that it fails to distinguish slightly finer bone in the rear legs as compared with the front ones. However, it does serve to remind us of the ideal for which to strive in our breeding efforts.

The numbered dotted lines in the accompanying figures indicate the measurements which can be made to determine the ratio of the various parts of the dog. All measurements are made without any allowance for coat. They are:

1. HEIGHT AT WITHERS: measured from the top of the shoulder blades to the ground.
2. LENGTH OF BODY: measured from the front of the chest (or point where the shoulder blade [scapula] and the upper arm join) to the back of the buttocks (tube iscium).
3. GIRTH OF BODY: measured around the thickest part of the chest just behind the front legs and withers.
4. LENGTH OF NECK: measured from the back tip of skull (occiput) to the withers.
5. LENGTH OF SKULL: measured from occiput (bony knob at back of skull between the ears—not prominent in the Schipperke) to the lowest point or front point of the stop (between the eyes).
6. LENGTH OF MUZZLE: measured from the front point of the stop to the end of the nose.

The ideal type was also portrayed by a charcoal drawing executed by M. Willy Anthoons, a Belgian sculptor now living in France, who was very well known on the Continent for his Schipperke objets d'art. This sketch was first introduced by the Royal Schipperkes Club (Belgium) and later reprinted by The Schipperke Club of America, Inc. It is presented here in *Figure 2*.

The ideal type portrayed by a charcoal drawing executed by M. Willy Anthoons, a Belgian sculptor who was very well known on the Continent for his Schipperke objets d'art.

117

Ch. Minette of Kelso was proclaimed as portraying the perfect breed type by M. R. Vander Snickt, eminent Belgian authority and former Secretary of the Royal Schipperkes Club, and the governing committee of the Royal Schipperkes Club in 1934.

While the aforementioned illustrations have their uses in fixing the correct Schipperke outline in the mind's eye, a good photograph more easily shows what the ideal Schipperke should be. Ch. Minette of Kelso was proclaimed as portraying the perfect breed type by M. R. Vander Snickt, eminent Belgian authority and former Secretary of the Royal Schipperkes Club, and the governing committee of the Royal Schipperkes Club in 1934. This photograph was also used to illustrate the 1934 booklet of the Royal Schipperkes Club.

THE HEAD

The head is one of the most important characteristics of the Schipperke and is often described as "foxlike." However, authorities of the breed agree that a proper Schipperke head should not be an exact likeness of the fox head but only *resemble* it, for there are marked differences. The muzzle of the fox is snipey, tapering to a very fine point in proportion to the head. The frontal bone, cheek bumps, and the muscles of the jaw under the skin are more prominent in the fox. The fox's expression is nervous, furtive, and rather frightened, while that of the Schipperke must be forthright, fearless, rather quizzical, alert, and attentive.

The cranium should be of medium width at the base, narrowing toward the muzzle. Narrow skulls are objectionable because they usually accompany overly long heads. Seen in profile with the ears laid back, the skull should appear very slightly rounded. Two major faults to avoid in this area are a flat or bulbous skull. The flat skull is seldom encountered in the Schipperke because the tendency in any small breed is for the forehead to be rounded. The rounded or domed

118

The fox's expression is nervous, furtive, and rather frightened while that of the Schipperke must be forthright, fearless, rather quizzical, alert, and attentive.

skull is a characteristic which tends to increase with a corresponding *decrease* in the size of the dog, to the point of forming the apple-head of the dwarf. Since the Schipperke is a relatively small breed, the domed skull is more to be feared, one of the more serious faults to affect a Schipperke, which is always accompanied by other faults, all typical of Toy dogs—round and prominent eye, deep stop, and a short muzzle pinched in under the eyes. Such faults give the dog a Pomeranian expression, quite untypical of the correct Schipperke.

Proportions

The stop, the perpendicular break between the forehead and muzzle located between the eyes, should be definite but not prominent. Since the head of the Schip should form a V-shape from the base of the skull to the tip of the nose, the muzzle must not be thick like a Chow's nor should it be pinched in under the eyes to make it thin and snipey. The upper jaw should be rather well filled in under the eyes so that the muzzle tapers smoothly and evenly to a small black nose. The lower jaw should be somewhat lighter than the upper, producing a slightly receding chin. It should not be square at its extremity, which can give a Bull Terrier appearance, nor should it be extremely pointed at the end to the extent of reproducing the snipey muzzle of the fox.

For proper proportion, the length of the muzzle from the tip of the nose to the stop should be slightly less than the length of the skull from the stop to the occiput. (Note: this point of measurement is *not* the same as designated in *Figure 1*. Instead, this is the midpoint of the stop.) The planes on the top of the muzzle

119

An example of a "Roman nose."

and the top of the skull should be perfectly parallel in the well-shaped head. However, when the ears are up in the alert position, the correct skull in profile will appear to be flat and rising slightly upward toward the ears. Occasionally, a Schipperke will have a curved muzzle bridge or "Roman nose," but *this is not desirable*.

The well-proportioned head should be symmetrical to the body. In general, short-bodied, thickset dogs should have a head which is pleasing to the eye and may have a slightly shorter muzzle. A rangy, larger dog may have a larger head with a longer muzzle.

Eyes

The ideal eye is small, more oval than round, dark brown, and placed more forward than sidewise. The eye should not be set obliquely in the head, for this tends to give a wolfish expression. Although the eye should be small and somewhat almond-shaped, the eye may assume a more rounded shape when the dog becomes excited and alert. The eye should not be sunken into the skull nor should it be a prominent or bulging eye. A light eye color is frequently seen in the Schipperke. This is a fault and is listed as such in the Standard, although breeders are divided in opinion as to the relative seriousness of this deviation from the ideal. Some Europeans consider it a major fault, and have advised that such individuals exhibiting this trait be discarded for breeding.

On the other hand, other authorities, including F. Isabel Ormiston, have stated that shape and expression are more important than color. This latter school

120

of thought regards the light eye, provided it is correctly shaped and well placed, as a much less serious fault than the large prominent eye of the preferred dark color. Yellow or black eyes are also a fault.

Ears

The ears of the Schipperke should be small. The shape of the ear should be triangular with the two sides of each ear being very nearly straight and meeting at the tip to form a sharp angle. The outer side of the ear should be the longest side, or hypotenuse, of the triangle in order for the ear to be carried properly. The ears should be placed high on the head so that they will come close together on top of the skull when the dog is excited or at full attention.

Various faults occur in the shape of the ear. The very narrow ear tends to be too long and is not of the correct small triangular shape required by the Standard. Another fault of the ear which may be seen are rounded tips, giving the appearance of being spoon-shaped. This is a deviation from the true triangle. The high ear placement required for the ideal is essential to produce the typical breed expression. A wide ear set is undesirable. It has been written that the Belgian authorities preferred the ears to be carried with a slight slant forward. The Standard sheds no light on this situation; it only states that the ears should be very erect.

Sometimes seen among Schipperkes are "drop" or floppy ears caused by weak cartilage. This is a disqualification. The cartilage must be sturdy enough to hold the ears upright. However, in very young puppies, the ears may be inclined to be floppy. The cartilage may not strengthen in some puppies until they are past the teething period.

The ears should be placed high on the head so that they will come close together on top of the skull when the dog is excited or at full attention.

Teeth

The Standard for the teeth of the Schipperke refers to the manner in which the front teeth, or incisors, of the upper jaw meet the incisors in the lower jaw when the mouth is closed. This is "the bite." When the incisors meet evenly, the upper teeth rest evenly on top of the lower ones, coming in contact like a pair of pincers forming a "level bite." In the "scissors bite" the upper front teeth tightly overlap the lower ones so that the teeth are in contact, fitting together like the two blades of a pair of scissors. Both bites are acceptable in the Schipperke.

There are two primary kinds of dentition faults: upper and lower prognathism. Upper prognathism or "overshot bite" occurs when the front teeth of the upper jaw project beyond those of the lower jaw so that they do not come in contact when the mouth is closed. Lower prognathism or "undershot bite" is the reverse condition in which the front teeth of the lower jaw project beyond those of the upper jaw. The amount of projection may occur in varying degrees from the point of just missing contact to an opening wide enough to allow the tongue to hang out when the jaws are closed. The Standard describes these conditions as faults when present to a slight degree, but disqualifications when pronounced. Many experienced breeders consider these faults very serious, as they are almost always hereditary and difficult to breed out. Authorities on breeding (all breeds) usually advise that dogs exhibiting these faults, particularly when pronounced, should not be used for breeding.

In addition to the above faults in the bite, irregularity in the placement of the incisors may sometimes occur, making it difficult to determine whether the bite is overshot or undershot. Some dental surgeons have stated that when only one of the front teeth extends over the other, it is an irregularity, but when two or more are out of place, prognathism is present. These irregularities can usually be avoided if care is taken to see that the baby teeth of the puppy are removed promptly before the permanent teeth break through the gums.

The well-proportioned head, accompanied by correctly shaped eyes and ears, will give the proper Schipperke expression as stressed by the Standard of the breed. This is often described as a keen, lively expression which may be mischievous and impudent but must never be mean or wild. The true Schipperke gives the impression of a wide-awake, alert, and energetic little dog interested in everything. The ideal expression contributes a large share to this overall effect.

THE NECK

The neck contributes significantly to the elegance and general balance of the Schipperke and so is of esthetic importance to the Schipperke silhouette. It should be strongly muscled and slightly arched with no sign of "throatiness," or superfluous skin under the throat.

Also of utmost importance is the carriage of the neck, which should be proud and animated, reminiscent of a spirited race horse. Such a carriage will show the slight arch of neck required. The alert dog will demonstrate a head carriage which appears to make the dog grow taller when excited and pulling up to attention. The correct length of neck will depend upon the length of the body, as it must be in balance to the rest of the dog for the correct silhouette. Although the neck will be correspondingly shorter in the very short dog, it must not be so short that there is no room for the slight arch required, nor so that the head appears set directly up on the shoulders. A full ruff will make the neck appear shorter and thicker than it is in actuality.

THE SHOULDERS

As in most breeds, the shoulder of the Schipperke should be well laid back. The shoulder blade or scapula should be attached to the rib cage in such a way that it slopes forward and down from the top of the withers, to form a sharp angle (as near as possible to 90 degrees) with the humerus or upper arm. The upper arm and shoulder blade should be of equal length. In this position, the scapula tends to be relatively long and broad so that the shoulder muscles are spread over a wider area. This will result in a sleek-appearing shoulder which flows freely and smoothly in motion. Thus, the desired sloping shoulder is very mobile and therefore produces the correct free-moving front legs so necessary for proper gait.

In the faulty straight shoulder, the scapula lies more upright over the ribs, thus forming a wider angle (not the desired 90 degrees) with the humerus. In this position, the scapula tends to be shorter and narrower so that the shoulder muscles are spread over a smaller area creating a more prominent bulge, which detracts from the beauty of the dog as well as the gait. This lack of sufficient angulation in the shoulder restricts the length of the front stride so that the front legs move with a short, stiff, and choppy gait.

THE FOREQUARTERS AND FEET

The front legs should be suspended in a perfectly straight line from the elbow and should be placed well under the body so that the chest appears as supported by the legs and not suspended between them. The leg bone should be in proportion to the size of the dog. The Schipperke is relatively fine in bone but not so fine as to appear weak. The short, cobby dog will usually be heavier in bone than a long, rangy one. The preferred bone has sometimes been described as medium or compact. Really fine bone and a cobby build are *not compatible* for true balance. On the other hand, coarse heavy bone is undesirable, especially in such a small breed, which should move with grace. The pastern should be

Too narrow.

Down in pastern.

Fiddle front.

Too wide, coarse feet.

FRONT FAULTS

Presented by The Schipperke Club of America, In Line Drawings by Christopher Gifford-Ambler

short, strong, and with a *slight* slope. Weak or spongy pasterns mar the silhouette and gait and are a fault. Frequently, toenails which are allowed to grow too long will cause a dog to be "down in pastern," and so it is wise to keep toenails trimmed short.

The feet should be small, round, and compact with strong, straight, and short, black toenails. The toes should be short, well arched, and held close together in order to form the ideal "cat-foot." The toes as well as the entire foot should point straight forward, turning neither out nor in. The pads should be tough and hard. A thin, splayed foot (toes spread apart) is an abomination. The hare-foot (long and narrow with close toes) and the too-large, coarse foot are undesirable although common. Too often, the conformation of the foot is over-looked both in breeding and judging, but it should be duly considered by the conscientious breeder. The small, compact cat-foot is an integral part of the beauty of the correct Schipperke silhouette.

THE BODY

The body of the Schipperke should be short and thickset—cobby, resembling a cob horse. The length of the back is measured along the spine from the withers to the pelvis. The body length is measured from the point where the scapula and the humerus join to the back of the buttocks. There are various deviations from the ideal, but two types are of concern to the exhibitor—the dog is short in body but lacks sufficient substance to be thickset or the dog is thickset but longer in body than desired. It is possible for the body to be short and the back relatively long, and this is especially true when the animal has a long loin. The reverse occurs when the back is short and the body is long. Careful study of the ideal proportions, as illustrated in the drawings, will aid the novice in developing an understanding of the proper relationship between the various parts of the body.

The topline of the Schipperke should be level or sloping slightly downward from the withers toward the rump when examined beneath the coat. The outstanding ruff adds to the appearance of the slope, making the dog seem noticeably higher at the withers than at the rear quarters. At the same time, the slope should not be so exaggerated as to make the rear quarters appear weak or shorter than the front quarters. The back should be strong and straight with no sag or roach. The sagging or sway back is a grave fault and is often accompanied by weak hindquarters, including cowhocks. Individuals with this weakness are not recommended for breeding.

In the ideal Schipperke, the chest must be broad with a deep brisket. The chest, or ribcage, encompasses that part of the body framework which is formed by the ribs. This does not include the shoulders. The brisket is comprised of the front portion of the chest which extends in front of the shoulders and down

Acceptable level back.

Sway-back.

High rump.

Roach-back.

BODY

This Schipperke has a tail which curls over the back. Some breeders also report that Schipperkes have been born with no tail, stub tails, and tails which are carried straight out from their bodies, like a labrador.

between the front legs and includes the deepest part of the ribcage just behind the front legs as well.

The Standard specifies that the ribs be well sprung. In cross section, the ideal Schipperke chest would appear as a modified oval with a relatively wide curve at the top and a narrow curve or rounded point at the bottom (sternum). Even so, the ribs should not be exaggerated in width to the extent that the chest becomes cylindrical or barrel shaped, or one that is typical of the Bulldog. An overly wide rib cage hinders the free movement of the front legs, which in turn affects correct gait.

The lower line of the chest should slope upward moderately but gracefully toward the abdomen with the abdomen correspondingly drawn up into a moderate tuck-up (the upward curve of the lower line of the loin). Though there should be a definite tuck-up, the abdomen must not be drawn up from the brisket in too pronounced an arc or the hindquarters will be too high, narrow, and weak—all negative features for the Schipperke. In addition, too much tuck-up may produce a roached back or give the suggestion of Whippet conformation. A Schipperke of the desired thickset build will not possess a pronounced waistline, though it should be perceptible. Also, a good coat will make the dog appear to have a more pronounced tuck-up than it has in actuality, particularly in dogs of small stature. The correct coat modifies the appearance of the Schipperke, and this fact must be considered when studying the ideal outlines illustrated here.

The rump must be broad and well rounded to compliment the required broad chest and to help form the thickset body. In no way should the rump of the Schipperke suggest a Fox Terrier minus a tail. However, the rear quarters should be very slightly narrower than the shoulder assembly—the heavier front

127

quarters being emphasized by the longer coat of the ruff, cape, and jabot. A closely docked tail adds to the "guinea pig" appearance necessary in a well-rounded rump. A narrow rear produces a too-pronounced "pear-shaped" body, with the hindquarters not in balance with the required thickset front.

The descriptive body term, "pear-shaped," seems to have been introduced by the English, as it was not used by the older Belgian and French authorities. Actually, this term is not applicable to the ideal Schipperke conformation, and it is a mistake to use it when describing the physical structure. Furthermore, this term is misleading for it tends to give the new fancier the idea that the breed should be narrower in the hindquarters than the Standard implies. "Pear-shaped" is the appropriate descriptive term for the Bulldog conformation, which is totally unlike that of the Schipperke.

The Schipperke is known as a tailless breed, and the breed Standard specifically states that no tail is visually discernible. However, this description is not meant to imply that the breed is born without a tail. As a matter of fact, most Schipperkes are born with full-length tails, although stub tails and occasionally no tail at all are seen in some families. A closely docked tail is necessary to provide the well-rounded rump described in the Standard.

THE HINDQUARTERS AND FEET

The hindquarters, which include the pelvic girdle, rear legs, and feet, should be somewhat narrower and lighter in bone than the front quarters yet strong and well-muscled in order to maintain balance with the required broad front. The thighs should be broad, long, and well-muscled with the stifle well bent but not extremely so as in the German Shepherd Dog. The hock joint should

Proper rear angulation plays an important role in producing the correct gait and the ideal silhouette.

have a sharp angle and the hocks should be short, referred to as hocks well let down—close to earth. Thus, the correctly formed rear leg will be well curved at the stifle, forming a fairly sharp angle at the hock *joint* with the hock itself then extending vertically downward to the foot.

The rear feet should be small, compact, and a bit smaller in size than the front feet, to correspond to the slightly lighter bone desired in the hindquarters. Viewed from the back, the pelvic girdle should be somewhat narrower than the shoulder assembly. The top leg bone (femur) should descend at a very small outward angle, but the lower portion of the legs below the knee (patella) should descend parallel to each other ending with the rear feet set the same distance

Cowhocked.

Toed-in, bandy-legged.

Straight stifles.

Over angulated.

REAR FAULTS

apart as the front ones. This formation gives the necessary square-set appearance of the well-constructed Schipperke.

Proper rear angulation plays an important role in producing correct gait and ideal silhouette. Seldom does too much angulation occur in the hindquarters, but its opposite, the straight stifle, does occur frequently. Straight stifles produce the same short, stiff, choppy movement in the rear as do the straight shoulders in the front, and these conditions are often seen together.

Other deviations are present when the rear legs do not fall in parallel lines below the knee. When the hocks or metatarsals (section from the hock *joint* to the foot) slant inward, the hock joint will point outward and the rear feet will turn inward, causing the dog to be pigeon-toed. This can exist both when the dog stands and moves. When its opposite occurs, the metatarsals slanting outward, the condition is called "cowhocks" and causes the hock joints to point inward and the feet to turn outward. Dogs exhibiting the weak, narrow, high hindquarters and/or cowhocks are not recommended for breeding. These are symptoms of a basic skeletal weakness which is extremely difficult to breed out of a line.

COAT

The coat on the Schipperke should be abundant, glossy, and resistant to the touch, rather harsh or crisp in texture, and should be short and fairly smooth on the ears, head, front of the legs below the elbow and hock joint. The coat should also be medium length on the body but decidedly longer behind the shoulders on the cape, around the neck on the ruff and extending down and back between the front legs on the jabot. It is also longer down the center of the back and on the rear of the thighs where it forms the culotte with the points turning inward. The culotte must be the same length as the ruff. One of the distinguishing characteristics of the correct Schipperke coat is a distinct differentiation between the length of the hairs in the ruff, cape, jabot, and culotte and those on the body, as well as the even shorter hairs on the ears, head, and lower legs.

Perhaps the most important word describing the coat is "abundant." Schipperkes must give the impression of being very furry individuals. The correct coat is a double one consisting of the longer, coarse, relatively harsh outer coat (guard hairs or top coat) and a shorter, softer, very dense undercoat. The undercoat is imperative because its density causes the ruff to stand out as required by the Standard.

There is nothing in the Standard stating that the coat should or should not stand out all over the body, as in the Keeshond, but it must be heavy enough to make the dog appear to have plenty of coat with both layers of the double coat easily discernible. The only requirement stated is that the ruff MUST stand out.

The most frequent faults are the long, silky coat and the short, harsh one. A silky or too-soft coat gives the Schipperke a sleek, shiny appearance which may be attractive but does not conform to the prototype. A more serious fault is

The coat should also be relatively short (medium length) on the body but decidedly longer behind the shoulders (cape), around the neck (ruff) and should extend down and back between the front legs (jabot).

the wavy coat which is seen occasionally, but, since this fault is visible at birth, it is easy to eliminate these dogs as breeding stock at an early age.

The complete absence of an undercoat, which causes an absolutely flat coat, is a serious fault. Such coats will often exhibit a definite parting of hair along the back like the Skye Terrier. Longer coats tend to be too soft and the harsh ones too short, although the longer coat provides the more correct general appearance. The ultimate goal is to breed dogs having the longer-length coat with the desired harsh texture.

Again, the decided difference in coat length between the body and the ruff

The dog in this photograph is a "fluff," a Schipperke with a soft, silky coat more than three inches in length. Note the head, which has a distinct "Toy" appearance.

131

and culotte should be emphasized. Some dogs having the desired longer coat, and also some with very short coats, have hairs of the same length all over with no differentiation between the length of the body coat, ruff, and culotte. *Lack of differentiation in coat length* should be *heavily penalized*, as such a dog lacks an essential breed characteristic.

A coat having no luster is not correct but is usually due to condition rather than an inherited factor. This condition often occurs during the periodic shedding process but may also appear as the result of poor nutrition, illness, or parasitic infestation. Many Schipperkes shed their coats twice a year, but some will shed only once a year and a few even less often.

The coat should be solid black in color. Although some authorities assert that the undercoat should also be jet black, many good-quality dogs show an off-black undercoat, with either a gray or charcoal cast to the color. If the *outward appearance* of such a Schipperke is jet black, the dog fulfills the requirement of the Standard, although some fanciers assert that an off-black undercoat is undesirable. Any permanent coat not having an overall jet black appearance is a definite disqualification, and such off-color dogs should not be used for breeding.

The undercoats of some Schipperkes take on a reddish tint or brown color at the approach of the shedding period. The outer or guardcoat may also take on a reddish tint or brown color due to sun bleaching during the summer months. These are transitory conditions, and the new coat will grow in as a natural black. In addition, certain parasitic infestations will also cause a brown or red, lusterless, rough coat in the Schipperke.

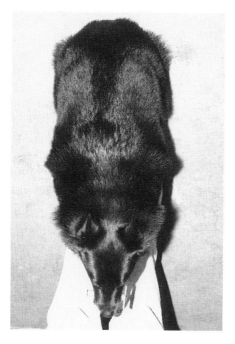

One of the distinguishing characteristics of the correct Schipperke is a distinct differentiation between the length of hair in the ruff, cape, jabot and culotte and those on the body. The hair is even shorter on the ears, head and lower legs.

SIZE

The size of the Schipperke is described in the Standard by linear measurements. The *suggested* height at the highest point of the withers is eleven to thirteen inches for males and ten to twelve inches for bitches. A Schipperke who falls outside of the linear measurements is *not* subject to disqualification.

On the average, most typical Schipperkes will range between 10 and 15 pounds, although there are exceptions. The very small dogs tend to have the characteristics of the Toy breeds such as the globular skull, round eyes, pinched-in muzzle, etc., rather than those typical for the breed. Conversely, the very large Schipperkes tend to be coarse or rangy like a Shepherd rather than the ideal short, square, thickset, and cobby dog with the relatively fine bone.

The Standard also applies a masculinity-femininity factor. Schipperke bitches are described as slightly smaller than the male. Males are decidedly masculine without coarseness. Bitches are decidedly feminine without overrefinement. If a Schipperke male and bitch of the same height were placed side by side and compared, the male should be slightly heavier in bone and build, whereas the female should have finer bone and features. Male Schipperkes usually have a heavier coat with a more pronounced ruff than a bitch. In other words, the male should look masculine and the bitch feminine. This factor has given rise to the terms a "bitchy dog" to describe the feminine dog and "doggy bitch" to describe the masculine bitch—both faults being considered undesirable in individuals used for breeding.

MOVEMENT

The revised Standard of the Schipperke, which became effective January 1, 1991, now includes a description of the proper gait (movement) of the Schipperke. Since the movement of the dog is determined directly by the anatomical structure and their relationship, gait truly becomes the test of structure. The gait of the Schipperke will spotlight any incorrect anatomic construction in the shoulder assembly, hindquarters, and body shape which might not be apparent by any other means.

The proper Schipperke gait is a smooth, well-coordinated, and graceful trot. When observed in profile, the Schipperke should move smoothly with the backline remaining level or sloping slightly downward from the shoulders to the rump. The front legs should move smoothly and flexibly in a medium stride forward with the feet clearing the ground freely but with no high stepping or "hackney action." The hind legs should propel the body forward with sufficient action in the leg joints to *prevent* a pitching or bounding motion to the backline. In this profile position, various structural faults manifested by the gait can be seen. If a dip appears in the mid-backline or if the rear quarters appear higher than the shoulders, incorrect shoulder or pelvic structure is evident. Short, choppy, and stilted movement is indicative of inadequate angulation of the rear legs.

When a moving Schipperke is viewed head on, the front legs should descend in a perfectly straight line from the elbows to the ground with the dog's feet the same distance apart as its elbows. The forelegs should move straight forward, parallel to each other at a slow trot. As speed increases there is a conversion toward centerline, but not a single track as in the German Shepherd Dog. Schipperkes should gait in an easy, flexible manner with no trace of paddling when the feet are alternately thrown to the side as in swimming, weaving with feet crossing over one another, or choppiness in the stride.

Paddling is caused when the dog's shoulder blades are fastened too tightly to the rib cage. This prevents the Schipperke from having freedom of motion. Conversely, loose shoulders allow the elbows to stick out sideways from the body with the corresponding toeing in of the feet. A rib spring too wide for the dog will also cause a dog to be "out at the elbows" and to have a rocking movement in gaiting. Although the feet must clear the ground easily, the Schipperke should not lift its feet in a high knee action like a hackney pony, as some Toy breeds often do.

When viewing a moving Schipperke "going away" or from the rear, the hind legs should move straight forward and parallel to each other in a free, smooth motion, forming a straight line from the hip through the hock to the pads with the rear feet pointing straight ahead.

The rear legs should move the same distance apart as the front ones. When they move too closely together, the dog looks off-balance. When moving too wide behind, the dog appears to waddle, an awkward motion. In a cowhocked dog, the hocks will move closer together than the rest of the rear legs. In extreme cases they may even touch and interfere with movement. In any degree, this fault is evidence of a basic weakness to be deplored. Its opposite is seen when the hocks are further apart than the rest of the rear legs and is often accompanied by turned in feet or "pigeon-toes." A straight but stiff movement results from straight stifles, a lack of sufficient angulation.

If the Schipperke lacks correct angulation, it cannot move with a correct gait. Unfortunately, the overly straight angulation of shoulder and/or stifle frequently accompanies the very short bodies so diligently sought by fanciers. To obtain this ideal, having the properly well-laid-back shoulder, correctly placed on the well-shaped, very short body, and finished off with a well curved stifle— all resulting in a flawless movement—is most difficult to attain and presents a real challenge to the conscientious breeder. However, once a beautiful gait is seen, it can never be forgotten. Its perfection is unmistakable; it is an esthetic joy to behold,—a transposition of motion into unforgettable poetry.

In studying the Standard, the Schipperke fancier must remember that it was written to describe a mature Schipperke. In applying its specifications to puppies and immature dogs, when selecting future breeding stock or show specimens, the examiner must exercise intelligent judgment, keeping in mind all the various stages of growth the puppy passes through on the way to maturity. Some faults appearing in the puppy may be lessened and/or corrected with maturity,

This dog illustrates many faults. There is no differentiation in coat length. The ears are too large and the stifles are straight. The body is long and lacks the desired thickset, "cobby" appearance.

and puppies exhibiting such imperfections could be retained for later evaluation. On the other hand, there are other faults which remain or become more severe with age so that Schipperkes exhibiting these faults could be ruled out for breeding or showing at an earlier age. Therefore, serious breeders must acquire the knowledge of these possible changes in puppy growth if they are to become proficient in selecting breeding and show stock successfully.

Schipperkes are seldom mature under two years of age. Neither the thickset body possessing the desired rib spring nor the ruff is well developed until then. Heavy bone and full size attained at six months usually predict a coarse, oversized adult. The best Schipperkes are those which mature slowly and remain puppyish and undeveloped under a year old. Caution is warranted before deciding against a promising puppy because it didn't develop as desired at one year of age.

The Standard of the Schipperke is designed to serve as a guide, not only for the show judge, whose duty it is to select the best specimens to be used to perpetuate the breed, but also for breeders and fanciers trying to improve the breed. As yet, the perfect dog has not been born but all serious breeders keep the dream alive that they can breed at least one very close to the ideal—a truly great one.

Schipperkes are wide-awake, alert, and energetic little dogs which are interested in everything that goes on around them.

9

The Schipperke Character

SCHIPPERKES have been described as large dogs in small bodies. They have the instincts of a guard dog—protective, devoted, courageous. They are also impish, active, and a bit of a devil.

The Schipperke is a utilitarian breed. At the time the breed was developed, dogs had to be useful in order to justify their existence. Just as the sheepdog is the guardian of herds and farm property, a smaller relative, the Schipperke, is the guardian of the household. In common with all guarding breeds, Schipperkes possess an inordinate sense of responsibility toward the home and everything in it and have an unshakable loyalty for the ones to whom they are devoted. Thus, a Schipperke may be slow to make friends and remains reserved or even indifferent toward strangers when the owner is not present.

Being small in size, the Schipperke is an ideal guardian to take the place of larger breeds for persons who do not have the space for a large dog. A Schipperke's curiosity is insatiable—a trait which helps create the perfect small watchdog. Nothing in the home escapes close inspection. It is not an uncommon experience for a Schipperke to thoroughly investigate each piece of furniture after a visitor has departed. With exceptionally keen hearing, no stranger can enter the Schipperke owner's house uninvited while the dog is within. Although too small to inflict much bodily harm, a piercing bark will make enough noise to scare away burglars and unwelcome strangers.

Likewise, a Schipperke will announce the arrival of callers with a sharp bark, then with a watchful eye and active nose examine each one as they enter the house. Each person is greeted in a characteristic way, depending upon whether he or she is known as friend, stranger, or personal enemy. The Schipperke is exclusive in all likes and dislikes.

Originally in Belgium, correct temperament was of major importance in judging. In 1882, a Belgian writer described the Schipperke temperament thus: "A little, all black devil, but minus the cloven hoof and the tail, such is the boatman's dog. A very demon for rats, mice, moles and everything that moves. An indefatigable watchdog, he rests neither day nor night, always on foot, attentive to everything that goes on within or without his dwelling; he does not weary of inspecting the house from cellar to garret and as soon as he observes anything amiss he warns his master by his piercing barks. He knows the ways of the family, mixes himself into everything and ends by thinking that he is the one who directs the household. His fidelity to his master is unalterable; his gentleness with children is equal to any test, but let the stranger beware if he lays a hand upon an object or a person; the Schipperke has teeth and can use them. A good stable dog, he is a great friend of horses and an excellent horseman. His happiness is to ride the broad-backed tow horse, then he struts, barking at passers-by for he would have them believe that he alone makes the boat go."

A Dutch fancier in the 1930s aptly described the breed as follows: "I have called [Schipperkes] "little devils." That they are, these little black rascals, nothing escaping their attention, ever watchful, always on the move, quick as water. [A Schipperke is] ever faithful to their master and mistress."

The Schipperke with a proper temperament is loving and loyal, never spooky or shy. Properly raised puppies soon learn the ways of the household, including who is permitted and who is not. Schipperkes give alarm when in their opinion, the situation is not quite right. Yet, the breed should not be so distinctly unfriendly as to snap at strangers without provocation.

The Schipperke is an avid ratter. The tendency is to worry prey, for a Schip will not only catch and kill but will sometimes also play with prey like a cat. There are some exceptions, of course. Just as individuals among hunting breeds vary in their prowess in the field, so do individuals among the Schipperke breed differ in their excellence as ratters. Some exhibit no instinctive skill in this respect, while others show superb natural ability in undiminished degree.

One breeder, located in a rural area, wrote that his Schipperke killed snakes, groundhogs, rats, gophers, and field mice. Another wrote that her house dog was a good ratter, kept snakes away from the house, rabbits out of the garden, and woodchucks out of the fields.

Years ago, F. Isabel Ormiston wrote about the ratting ability of some of her Schipperkes. Her first import, Flore de Veeweyde, was an excellent ratter. One night, when Miss Ormiston went up to her room, she found a recently slain rat neatly stretched out on a pillow. Flore, considering this a most precious morsel, had presented it as a most valuable gift to an owner to whom she was completely devoted. Miss Ormiston also described the rat-catching accomplish-

A Schipperke on horseback, perhaps just as European ancestors rode the backs of the barge horses that pulled the barge back up the river in Belgium.

Schipperkes are ratters as illustrated by Am/Can U-CDX Midnight Meadows Cinderella, Am UD, Can CDX shown here at age ten years with a mole she caught.

ment of her first homebred champion: "Ch. Reine Claude of Kelso is one of the best ratters I have ever seen, having hundreds to her credit. Last year she caught and killed one that was so extraordinary in size that farmers came from miles around to see it, many claiming it was the largest rat they ever saw. It met its end in a peculiar way. I had entered the car, taking Claude with me, and started the engine. Rats are extraordinarily fond of engine oil, and often climb into the engine, making their way in through the underbody and lick the oil in the drip pan. This one evidently did so, for when I started the engine he leaped out. Claude flew out the window and had him by the back of the neck in a second; one good shake and his neck was broken."

Another fancier described a Schipperke's ratting ability at sixteen years of age: "His lips were grey and he had not a single tooth left, which did not prevent him from chasing rats, only, no longer being able to bite them, he held them to the ground until someone came and gave them the 'coup de grace'!''

SCHIPPERKES ABROAD—A HISTORY OF HUNTING

Although the Schipperke has been noted for a natural ability to destroy rats, mice, and other vermin, they can also be used for certain other kinds of hunting. The Belgians report that the Schipperke makes an excellent hunting dog

Schipperkes are a utilitarian breed. This Schipperke was used to hunt pheasant. His owner claimed "Skipper" was the best hunting dog he had ever owned.

140

and was often used for that purpose in times past. They certainly have an exceedingly keen nose for scenting and can trail readily in an unrivaled manner. Mr. Georges du Bosch wrote about a Schipperke in a letter to *Chasse Et Pêche* in the beginning of the century: "It seems to me that people forget that the Schipperke is not only handsome and pleasing and an excellent watchdog, but he is also a first rate terrier, a hunting dog di primo cartello. The Schipperke is actually the natural companion and obliging helper of the ferret. He is a remarkable rabbit dog . . . I even know one who covers the field like a setter and points partridge! I have not seen him at work only once but one hundred times; it is my keeper's dog. At work, this Schipperke is surprising. When he doesn't call— that is, after having taken up the scent at the warrens, he does not give a low bark—it is useless to put in the ferret, the ground is deserted. Never have I seen this intelligent little dog mistaken. In the fir groves, he traces the rabbit from tree to tree, running like a Dachshund and giving voice like a Basset Hound. It seems to me that if one wants to take the trouble to restore the original race of Schipperkes, it is as well to develop their pleasing qualities and their working talents together."

THE WORKING SCHIPPERKE IN THE UNITED STATES

Various tales of the Schipperke's capacity for successful hunting have been told in the United States. In the 1930s, Mr. Culbertson of Minnesota wrote that his Schipperkes were excellent squirrel and rabbit dogs and added that he hunted with them regularly. Moreover, he depended on them to dispose of woodchucks and the like on his property. Another fancier living within city limits testified to dogs energetically searching for and chasing rabbits out of the garden.

A breeder told of using a Schipperke for hunting. He wrote: "I could write a book on my experiences with the Schipperke in hunting pheasants. For that purpose the Schipperke so outclasses any other hunting dog bred that it puts them in a super class by themselves. I could write many pages about my experiences with the little Skipper following up after hunting dogs had finished. I have gone over the same field afterwards with the little tailless wonder dog and got my limit of birds."

Having been bred for centuries for usefulness as a guard and ratter (all traits requiring independent action on the part of the dog), the Schipperke is inclined to be a bit headstrong, sometimes stubborn, certainly exercising an independent will. This characteristic may make the dog somewhat less tractable than some of the larger working breeds, but such are the characteristics of clever children. And the Schip is clever. Nevertheless, this independence is not a real disadvantage to the breed and lends attractiveness and impishness to his very individual personality.

Schipperkes are intelligent and quick to learn. This has been demonstrated time and again by the excellent results Schipperkes have achieved in Obedience work. Complete devotion to the owner provides the desire to please that person. For this reason various trainers have found Schipperkes to be extremely adaptable to education. In fact, it is not unusual to find a Schipperke showing in the conformation ring and Obedience ring in the same day!

This intelligence, coupled with a keen sense of hearing, gives the Schipperke the ability to perform as "hearing ear" dogs for the deaf. Schipperkes have been trained to distinguish between telephone calls, door bells, alarm clocks, and the approach of people and inform their owner of such sounds.

Schipperkes living in the country have driven milk cows to and from the pasture without special training. One small Schip tended a goat herd, taking them to pasture and later bringing them back—in fact doing everything a regular herd dog would do.

Other Schipperkes have been used as narcotic detection dogs, messengers in wartime, therapy dogs for handicapped children and geriatric patients, and trick dogs performing in circuses and traveling shows. One Alaskan Schipperke was even employed to pull a drag line through underground culverts for the purpose of rewiring worn-out heater cores!

In addition to the practical attributes of the breed, the required disposition for the Schipperke is to be curious, courageous, and energetic—an altogether active and indefatigable spirit. Schipperkes of dull temperament, which show no interest in things around them, lack proper temperament. Schipperkes should be

Schipperkes are charmers and will often captivate onlookers by "pattycaking" as demonstrated by Learjet's Dream on Striker.

right up on their toes, pugnacious with other dogs nearby and missing nothing that goes on. These should be personality plus even to the extent of being slightly rebellious.

The curiosity and hunting ability of the Schipperke have often been an undoing. When someone has been careless and left a door or gate ajar, the Schipperke will dash off, looking for those delightful smells, or perhaps a mouse or other rodents. Hunting is the Schipperke's favorite pastime. By the time they are tired of the hunt, it may be two days later and ten miles from home.

Some Schipperkes have amusing traits, such as patty-caking. These dogs will sit up and wave their front paws like a Prairie Dog outside its hole. Because this habit usually fascinates a human audience, the Schipperke soon learns to employ this trick to beg effectively for something or seek forgiveness.

Other Schipperkes are great diggers, digging deep holes in the middle of open ground like a woodchuck. Mr. Arin of France reported that a small bitch of nine pounds dug a hole 6½ feet deep in stony soil. The Belgian import, Ch. Bebe de Ter Meeren of Kelso, was in the habit of digging a hole of six to eight feet in length with a circular roomlike den of three to four feet in circumference at the end. However, only a few individuals with such unusual digging accomplishments have been described, although many Schipperkes do like to do some digging, especially when engaged in seeking out ground-living varmints.

THE SCHIPPERKE AS A COMPANION

The Schipperke is an ideal house dog. As a whole, the breed is clean in habit, small enough to live happily in the small quarters of an apartment, economical to maintain, and very healthy. One of the most enjoyable aspects of the Schipperke physique is that the breed has no doggy odor, which is so disagreeable in some other breeds. Thus, they do not need frequent bathing nor are they objectionable in odor during rainy weather when their coats become damp from an outing. Most Schipperkes are also easily housebroken.

Because as incurable busybodies Schipperkes find many distractions within the house, they need very little outside exercise to keep in good physical condition and good health. It must be kept in mind, though, that the Schipperke must maintain an active way of life, whether in a city apartment or a country estate. They delight in a wild race after birds when they fly low to the ground on a warm summer's day, in wild charges after the neighbor's cat which has imprudently entered the garden, and in interminable pursuit of small pests which move. But the Schipperke loves best of all to be with loved ones in whatever activity they enjoy.

As a companion, the Schipperke is completely devoted, loyal and loving to family. They often become attached to one person, but remain faithful and affectionate to all loving members of the family. Nothing delights Schipperkes more than to be with their owners for everything; be it a long rambling hike in the country, a leisurely walk on a city sidewalk, or even an idle day spent reading quietly.

Children and Schipperkes are natural companions. Though gentle with youngsters and babies in the family, this little dog becomes an unswerving protector at the approach of any perceived danger.

The common belief that the Schipperke is yappy and inclined to snap is without foundation. There may be some individuals with such faults, but it is not characteristic of the breed as a whole. As a rule Schipperkes are among the best-behaved dogs at shows. Any kennel is apt to be noisy at times, but individually owned Schipperkes are usually as quiet as any other breed of guard dog. Excessive barking for no reason comes from poor early training. It is necessary to train any dog to be a good citizen, regardless of the breed.

Schipperkes have no inferiority complex and are unsurpassed watchdogs, unexcelled companions, and superlative ratters, and are adaptable at home, on a boat, in an apartment, on a ranch, and love to travel. They are as agile as a mountain goat and therefore excel in Agility Training. By these traits, the Schipperke has earned a nickname which has been attached to the breed for many, many years. Today still, the Schipperke is affectionately called the "little black devil."

10

Care and Health
of the Schipperke

THERE ARE many good publications available regarding the general care of dogs. This chapter is not meant to take the place of a comprehensive study of dog care, but rather it is meant to assist the Schipperke owner in developing a blueprint of care with the Schipperke specifically in mind.

FOOD AND NUTRITION

There are excellent books and pamphlets currently available to the general public regarding proper nutrition of dogs. In addition, veterinarians, breeders, and many other dog owners are generally happy to share their knowledge with a new owner. This is not meant to be a comprehensive course in canine nutrition. It is intended as a guide in developing the optimum feeding program for the Schipperke. Therefore, the information presented here is somewhat simplified.

The dog's basic need is protein in addition to vitamins and minerals. Marketed dog foods contain fat ranging from 2 to 9 percent. A variety of foods used to be required to include all the elements necessary for good nutrition. Today's vastly improved dog foods have removed the need to combine many foods.

Federal law mandates that all dog foods must clearly state the ingredients and nutritional contents on the label. In addition, most manufacturers also give the vitamin and mineral content as compared to standard daily requirements. All dog foods must state the percentage of protein. There are various kinds of proteins, all of them necessary for a balanced diet. Most dry dog foods contain the required amount of protein; more, in fact, than only plain meat.

Canned dog food is usually 74 percent water and may contain less than half as much protein as the dry types. From an economic standpoint, dry food is usually less expensive per serving than canned food.

Some fanciers may find that Schipperkes do better with the addition of more protein from animal sources. Others prefer to mix a small amount of canned food into a dry food base, still others will add an occasional *cooked* egg, a sprinkling of nonfat dry milk, or a small amount of lean ground meat. Lean beef *may* be fed raw but poultry or pork should be cooked. Never feed a Schipperke any pork or poultry still attached to the bone, as these bones are brittle and form sharp splinters which can perforate a dog's intestinal tract with fatal results.

A controversy exists regarding snacks. Schipperkes are engaging and charming characters and often beg for tidbits, especially at mealtime. A piece of cooked or raw vegetable is an acceptable treat. Peas, corn, or other *husked* vegetables may cause a blockage of the intestine. Table scraps should not become a substitute for regular meals.

Fresh water is essential to the health of any dog. It aids in digestion and protects the tissues of the body from dehydration; therefore, it must be readily available to the Schipperke at all times.

Feeding the Puppy

There are a variety of dog foods which have been specially formulated to meet the nutritional needs of a growing puppy. Schipperke puppies may consume as much food per day as a grown dog. Some breeders prefer to have food available to the puppies at all times while others prefer to divide the young puppy's food into three or four meals a day. The amount of food will vary with each individual puppy.

A reputable breeder should furnish a diet with each puppy. Follow it as closely as possible since a sudden change may cause an upset. If a change is desired, it should be done gradually and only after the pup has become thoroughly acclimated.

During the first few days of ownership, some puppies exhibit a slight loss of appetite. This may be caused by stress and the sudden upset in his way of life. If the loss of appetite continues beyond two or three days, or if the puppy develops loose stools or an elevated temperature (normal temperature for a dog is 101.6), the puppy should be examined by a veterinarian and the breeder notified of the results.

Feeding the Adult Dog

At nine to eighteen months of age, the young Schipperke may have the quantity of food reduced (if free fed) or may be placed on two meals per day. During this same time period, many breeders gradually switch the young dog to a food formulated to meet the needs of an adult dog. This may be accomplished by gradually adding adult dog food to the puppy formula with each successive meal until the young dog is eating the adult formula.

After eighteen months, many dogs do well on one meal per day, although this is not absolute. There are many Schipperkes who eat two meals per day all their lives. The key is to regulate the food intake so that the dog maintains a healthy weight, neither too fat nor too thin.

Feeding the Stud Dog and Pregnant Bitch

A stud dog should be kept in prime condition. However, it is unlikely that any Schipperke stud is so heavily used that he requires a special diet. If in doubt, consult a competent veterinarian.

It is important that a Schipperke bitch be healthy and in good physical condition *prior* to mating. After conception, she should be fed one of the numerous diets on the market specially formulated for the pregnant bitch. (See Chapter 13)

GENERAL CARE

All dogs require a certain amount of grooming to keep the dog clean and comfortable and help maintain basic good health. The owner of a Schipperke is fortunate to own a dog which requires a minimum of grooming care. The well-groomed Schipperke can attract favorable attention and serve as a public advertisement that the owner cares.

Brushing

The primary requisite for a good healthy coat is a healthy dog. The Schipperke should have a combination of a good, well-balanced diet, adequate exercise, and freedom from parasites of all kinds. There is no substitute for daily brushing, which will keep the coat in clean, top notch condition. This operation should be done with a medium-hard brush having stiff bristles which remove both surface dirt and loose dead hairs.

Brushing should be done *first against* the lay of the hair, especially around the neck and on the chest, and *then with* the lay of the hair. It gives a better finish to the appearance of the Schipperke if the ruff and jabot are finally brushed

Ch. Brad Crundwell of Jet-O, winner of multiple Group placements, including several Group Firsts. He won Group First at Del Monte Kennel Club at ten years of age. This dog is an example of how excellent care and good grooming, when combined with the right genes, can produce an outstanding dog. *Ludwig*

forward against the lay of the coat. Some breeders also recommend a brisk all-over massage of the skin with the fingertips prior to the brushing session to invigorate the skin and stimulate oil secretion. Frequent and regular massage followed by brushing also removes most of the dirt and dead hairs so that the need for frequent bathing is nullified.

Shedding

Schipperkes shed very little most of the year, but can lose their undercoat or guard coat all at once. This can occur seasonally or hormonally, as in the case of a bitch preceding the heat cycle. Some Schipperkes may also "blow" their coat when placed under anesthesia or during an illness. Still others will lose their coats because of heavy worm infestation.

148

The shedding period of the Schipperke calls for some changes in the grooming routine. During this process, the undercoat will come loose in thick bunches and will make the dog uncomfortable. At this time, the owner should also use a metal comb with teeth set moderately far apart—one specifically designed for dogs.

Take it easy when combing out these clumps of dead hairs. Though the hair may be loose, rough combing may cause the dog pain. Schipperkes seem to appreciate the careful removal of the dead hairs, which can cause discomfort, irritation, and itching. Neglecting the coat at this stage can cause the dog to resort to scratching. Excessive scratching will not only be annoying to the owner but may injure the skin and give rise to various skin ailments and infection. If the Schipperke continues to scratch and bite at the skin after shedding has stopped, and close examination reveals no sign of external parasites or skin disease, dry skin is probably the cause. Dandruff and dry skin commonly accompany the shedding process, and the presence of dandruff is a sure sign of dryness. This condition can be largely overcome by regular application of oil to the skin or oil added to the diet if none is ordinarily used. Baby oils can be used, but commercial oil preparations which are specifically designed for use on dogs are better.

When the dog is shedding, a quick way to get the dog back in coat is to get the old coat out. A good warm bath and strong blow dryer forces the dead coat out. The new coat comes in quicker and does so in about six to eight weeks. Misting several times per day with ice water helps also.

Bathing

Because the Schipperke has a harsh top coat which tends to shed dirt and is free of offensive doggy odor, there is seldom a real need to give the Schipperke a complete bath. However, a bath is not harmful, provided a mild soap is used followed by a thorough rinsing. The dog should then be kept in a warm, draft-free place until completely dry right down to the skin.

There have been many statements over the years on why Schipperkes should not be bathed. Arguments against bathing include that bathing destroys natural oils, softens coat, causes dandruff, is not good for them, and so many others that one tends to forget. If a Schipperke is healthy, the skin produces natural oils on a daily basis so the hair and skin are replenished regularly. A bath with a strong soap can burn the skin or cause an allergic reaction. This can be avoided by using a gentle soap or shampoo.

Shampoos will not soften a coat. The hair shaft of a Schipperke is grooved and will collect minute particles of dirt. This may make the coat feel stiff. When washed, the dirt is removed from the hair shaft, leaving a clean, soft, incorrect, coat. If the coat is correct, it will feel like a clean, correct coat when shampooed. Dandruff is dry skin or the skin shedding in layers. A sudden change of climate (usually dry) can trigger a case of dandruff as can improper diet or illness.

Bathing cleans pores, removes dead coat, and makes the coat look and feel healthy.

If the Schipperke begins to leave soiled spots on furniture, woodwork, or bedding, and bathing is not possible, various other cleansing methods can be used. There are commercially available dry shampoos made for dogs. These are brushed deeply into the coat of the dog, then out again. Another method is a liquid shampoo, which requires no rinsing but does require *careful* and thorough drying. The drying period is shorter than that needed after giving a regular bath because the dog is not wet clear down to the skin. This is particularly useful in the winter when wet bathing might prove difficult.

To freshen a coat and remove grime, four to five drops of creme rinse can be placed in a quart of water, dipped on a washcloth, and vigorously rubbed through the coat. This will clean the coat, making it feel fresh and smell good.

If care is taken, even a young puppy may be bathed when the need arises. Otherwise, it is recommended that a puppy not be given a bath under five or six months of age.

Hot Weather

A word of caution! It is sometimes believed that clipping off the coat in hot weather will make a dog cooler. Nothing is further from the truth. *Do not* clip off all the coat of your dog unless he has some overall skin trouble which demands such treatment. Shearing off the coat makes the dog susceptible to various skin ailments and insect bites from which his natural coat protects him. It deprives him of his natural insulation against the heat. With all his coat, the average Schipperke suffers less from hot weather than some of the short-coated breeds.

Toenails and Feet

The grooming routine includes the care of other parts of the dog as well as the coat. Regular care of the feet, teeth, eyes, and ears must also be followed to keep Schips looking and feeling their best.

The Schipperke's toenails should be kept *short*. Untrimmed nails grow long and pointed. Long nails often are a source of misery to the dog by spreading the toes out to unnatural positions and forcing the dog to walk on the back of the feet, thus being off balance when moving. This situation can cause soreness of the feet and possibly lameness. Not only may these long nails scratch the members of the family when playing or handling their pet, but they may also catch in looped naps of rugs, carpets, and upholstery. When clipping or filing the nails down to correct length, care must be taken not to injure the dog by cutting into the quick. For the owner who has not learned to do this chore, it is an easy and inexpensive matter to have a groomer or in some cases veterinarian do this. If the Schipperke's dewclaws were not removed, make certain that the dewclaw nail is well trimmed.

150

Some Schipperkes grow long unsightly hairs between the pads of their feet. Though it is not absolutely necessary to trim off these hairs, such trimming does provide the dog with a neater looking foot and reduces the amount of moisture and dirt the dog would otherwise track into the house.

Teeth

The teeth should be kept clean and free of tartar. Tartar forms on the teeth of some dogs earlier and more rapidly than on others. This deposit should be removed whenever it forms in order to prevent unpleasant breath and to avoid the premature loss of teeth.

A Schipperke's teeth can be kept free of tartar by regular brushing or scaling. If a young dog's teeth are cleaned on a regular basis, it may not be necessary to have then cleaned by a veterinarian. If excessive tartar builds up, and the dog will not permit the owner to clean the teeth, the veterinarian will have to anesthetize the dog in order to clean and polish the teeth. Polishing smoothes the surfaces of the teeth and minimizes future tartar formation. Between scaling operations the teeth can be cleaned by wiping with a damp cloth dipped in a mixture of equal parts table salt and soda (bicarbonate of soda). Such cleaning will slow the process of tartar deposit. Chewing on hard "Nylabones," rawhide, or large natural bones that will not splinter may also be helpful.

Eyes

Although the Schipperke is not particularly susceptible to eye troubles, the eyes should also be checked regularly. The eyes are subject to the irritation of foreign objects just as are human eyes. When the dog romps through tall grasses and weeds, small seeds may fall into the eyes and cause painful irritation.

Another source of irritation which gives rise to the same condition is the wind from which airborne dirt particles may blow into the eye, especially if the owner allows riding in an automobile with the dog's head outside the window. This is a dangerous practice!

A watering eye indicates something is wrong! If this occurs, the eyes may be gently rinsed out with mild saline solution, followed by the application of some canine eye ointment. Boric acid solution commonly used for an eye wash has been found to have poisonous effects when absorbed or taken internally. It should not be used! Watery eyes accompanied by a runny nose and/or fever indicate disease. For this and any other eye trouble, consult your veterinarian.

Ears

The ears of a Schipperke seldom cause trouble. However, they too, should be checked periodically. A foul-smelling, thick brown substance in ear canals may indicate the presence of ear mites. An infestation of parasites can cause severe discomfort to the Schipperke, infections and even deafness. A veterinarian should be consulted immediately and the prescribed medication should be used according to direction. Another problem which may occur are fly bites. In areas where there is livestock, flies may land on the exposed ear and bite, drawing blood. The scent of blood will often attract more flies, thus creating a vicious cycle to the Schipperke. There are many commercial preparations on the market which can be applied to the Schipperke's ears and will repel these pests.

In the Schipperke, we have the hardiest of all small dogs. With its close undercoat, the coat is strongly resistant to wind and rain but is not long enough to be troublesome. This is a dog that can sleep without heat in an ordinary winter if provided with a draft-free shelter. A Schip fares just as well in a heated home or apartment. One important point to emphasize is that a dog should not be shifted to live outdoors without heat during cold weather after becoming adjusted to a heated home. This can produce dire consequences. A draft-free shelter in bad weather is a must for any breed and particularly so for Schipperkes. While they can stand a very considerable amount of cold, they will often develop a husky cough if exposed to very strong, cold wind for any length of time. Otherwise this is a rugged healthy dog with a remarkable record for a long life span. Schipperkes frequently live to be twelve to fifteen years old and even older. Several have lived to be seventeen and eighteen and one imported from Scotland lived to be twenty-one years old. The record so far known for the breed is given in the book, *Dogs in Britain* by Clifford L. B. Hubbard printed in 1948, which told of a Schipperke owned in Holt, Norfolk (England), being twenty-four years old when it died in January 1933.

It cannot be emphasized enough that it is *not cruel* to prohibit a Schipperke from roaming freely. Confinement prevents the dog from being run over, poisoned, or exposed to various diseases. The Schipperke is small enough to get required exercise in the house or a dog run and can easily be trained to walk on a leash. Daily walks are good for dog and owner. The bitch in heat, who is not permitted to exercise outside her own pen, may not attract neighborhood males. However, she should be watched carefully so that an unplanned pregnancy does not occur.

HEALTH PROBLEMS

Although the Schipperke is relatively free of major health problems, there are some problems within the breed owners should be aware of.

Coughing

Some bloodlines of Schipperkes seem to be prone to a chronic cough, which is often aggravated when a training collar is placed around the neck. This cough should not be confused with ''kennel cough,'' a contagious viral infection.

The cause of the cough seems to be related to the structure of the trachea of the individual Schipperke.

Cryptorchidism

This is the absence of testicles or the failure of the testicles to descend into the scrotum. Researchers generally agree that it has a genetic basis, most probably as a sex-limited recessive trait. However, the method of inheritance has not been conclusively proven by the test breeding of affected dogs or suspected carriers, and their progeny. Environmental and physical factors also may have a bearing on the condition.

There are two types of cryptorchidism. The bilateral cryptorchid has neither testicle present in the scrotum. They may be retained in the inguinal canal. The unilateral cryptorchid has one retained testicle and one that is in the scrotum. This is frequently called a monorchid, but the word is accurate only when referring to a dog with one testicle, no matter where the location.

As for the individually affected dog, the majority of veterinary practitioners have little success in trying to correct the condition with hormone therapy. In some instances surgery may bring the testicles into normal position. This, of course, cannot correct the genetic flaw, and surgically corrected cryptorchids should not be used for breeding and may not be shown. Surgical removal of retained testicles is recommended in the great majority of cases because of the danger of malignant tumors.

Epilepsy

Epilepsy has become more common in the Schipperke breed. Some forms of epilepsy are hereditary and can be passed on from generation to generation. Other forms are caused by a brain injury. The symptoms of epilepsy can range from a blank stare lasting several seconds to a full seizure where the dog is straining and incapacitated. In the event of a full seizure, the dog should be watched and talked to in a calm and soothing voice until the seizure has ended. A seizure may last many minutes. If an owner suspects epilepsy, a veterinarian should be consulted. Diagnosis may be difficult because many veterinarians are not able to confirm epilepsy without witnessing a seizure. There are prescription medications available which will help control seizures.

Fungus Infections

In the grown dog, the most common ailment, and one of the most difficult to conquer, is a fungus infection. The Schipperke seems particularly susceptible, and certain bloodlines evidence it more than others. Bare patches of skin usually appear during hot, damp weather, but it can flare up in the dead of winter. Consult your veterinarian first to be certain it is not something else. Bactine, a human antiseptic and fungicide, is often helpful. Allergy shots may provide some relief but usually only temporarily. Some breeders have had excellent results in curing this ailment with Desenex, either in powder or liquid form, which is a human fungicide now available at your drugstore. Avoid any product with an oily base. Make certain that any topical cream used is not poisonous, as many dogs will often lick the affected area clean.

Legg-Perthies Disease

Legg-Perthies disease is seen sporadically in dogs of the smaller breeds. No evidence of the condition's heritability is recognized. The condition is only seen during adolescence, often in precocious puppies. Loss of adequate blood circulation to the femural head (the ball of the ball-and-socket hip joint) results in its deformity as it literally erodes away. By the time the dog exhibits much discomfort, the process is ended or nearly so. This process is followed by healing with surgical reformation of the misshapen femoral head and neck, which results in chronic gait abnormalities and eventual arthritis of the hip.

Parasites

There are various kinds of intestinal worms and a different treatment for each. In order to treat the Schipperke properly the worm must first be identified. Take a sample of the fresh stool to your veterinarian every six months for a proper diagnosis.

Fleas should not be tolerated! They carry diseases and are a host for tapeworm. If a dog ingests a flea, the eggs of the tapeworm will hatch inside the intestinal tract. When using flea products on a Schipperke, it is recommended that less toxic products labeled "safe for cats" be used.

Preventative medications are available for heartworms. Heartworms can only be identified by testing blood samples. Medication should only be given upon advice of a veterinarian, as it can prove fatal if given to a dog who has heartworm.

Vaccinations

All dogs need routine vaccinations and regular health checkups. The schedule of these routine vaccinations depends on the age of the dog and the number of vaccinations required. The requirement for a rabies innoculation varies from state to state.

11

Showing the Schipperke in Conformation

T HE PRIMARY PURPOSE of conformation classes at any dog show is to select those individuals that are judged to best represent the ideal Schipperke as described by the Standard. Judging in the United States is done by comparison. The dogs are first compared to the breed Standard, then against the others in the ring. Only dogs who are entered in the show are allowed in the ring. Entries must be received by the proper dog show superintendent on or before the closing date listed on the entry form.

The Schipperke's coat should be clean and free from foreign substances. The teeth should be cleaned, and toe nails clipped and filed three or more days before the show. The dog should be bathed before the show, then groomed with a soft brush to restore the natural oil in the coat. The dog's whiskers may be trimmed if desired.

On the day of the show, the exhibitor should arrive at the show grounds at least an hour before ring time. This will give the dog an opportunity to get acquainted with the surroundings. If time permits, the ring in which Schipperkes will be judged should be located and the judging procedure observed. About one-half-hour prior to ring time, the Schipperke should be gone over for final touch-up and allowed the opportunity to urinate and defecate.

Schipperkes at a benched show in 1950. Benched shows require the dogs entered to be present on the bench for viewing by the public during certain times. Although common in the 1950s, the benched show has all but disappeared today with only a few remaining in the U.S.

JUDGING

Some exhibitors carry their dogs when outside the ring so there is no possibility of someone stepping on the dog's feet. Once the ring is entered, however, the dog must be standing squarely and showing. When the dogs first enter the ring, some judges request exhibitors to wait until everyone is present before posing or ''stacking'' their dogs. This allows the dogs and their exhibitors to settle down, and gives the judge a chance to check for readily apparent faults, such as sway back, poor hindquarters, lack of coat, and most important, alertness and expression.

Once everyone is in the ring, the judge will often walk down the row of Schipperkes, looking for the small, thickset, alert, all-black dog, possessing a silhouette which is unlike that of any other breed. Care should be taken at this time so that your dog is posed in a natural position, although care should also be taken to present the best possible picture of the dog. For example, if the exhibitor is stretching the dog to cover a low shoulder fault, it is better to spread the dog's rear legs. A Schipperke posed in a stretched position never looks natural. Never expect any Schipperke to hold a pose for too long at one time.

Next, after gaiting around the ring, the dogs are set up for individual examination. Many judges will request that the Schipperke be placed on an

156

Schipperkes on the bench at the Golden Gate Kennel Club show in 1976.

examining table. The judge then goes over each Schipperke from nose to rear. When examining the head, particular attention is given to the eyes, which should be very dark brown and oval in shape; the ears, which should be small, pointed, and held erect and as close together as possible on the top of the head; and the bite, which should be level or scissors.

The front legs are examined for straightness and bone, which should not be too heavy. The feet should be compact and firm like a cat's foot, with short nails. The chest should be broad with plenty of coat forming a jabot. There must be an undercoat, and the texture should be such that the coat feels slightly harsh to the touch and not smooth or velvety. Distinctive features of the Schipperke coat are plenty of long hair around the neck forming a ruff, a semicircular overlay of long hair on the back over the shoulders known as the cape, and plenty of long hair on the hindquarters forming what are called culottes. In examining the hindquarters, the judge looks for hocks parallel to the ground, correct angulation of the legs, and in the case of males, determines that the dog has two testicles properly descended into the scrotum.

After the individual examination is completed, each dog is gaited individually. Gait is very important in the show ring, as it reveals the soundness of the animal. The gait should be smooth and steady, without paddling or interference. The true Schipperke gait is smooth and even and in no way resembles that of a Terrier or Toy dog. The hind feet follow directly behind the front ones, with a tendency toward single tracking as the speed increases. The exhibitor should know at which speed a dog moves best and stick to that speed while in the show ring.

Lara Luke, and her junior handling dog, Ch. Jetstar's Touchdown, winning Best Junior Handler at the SCA National Specialty in 1986. *Booth*

There are few dogs in any breed that gait as well going and coming, at the same speed. The sound dog will look good at all speeds. Dogs with very open angles in the front assembly, steep shoulder blades, or poor angulation in the rear legs, should not be gaited too fast. If they are, the dog will move both front and rear legs in a short, choppy gait.

Some dogs will gait better on a loose lead than on a tight one. A dog with a short neck usually gaits better if the head is not held too high. The exhibitor must decide which fault to cover. Most judges like to see a dog gaited on a loose lead. The dog then moves naturally and the judge is able to see structural faults indicated during the manual examination.

Lastly, the dogs are posed again. The judge studies the silhouettes and compares each dog with the others. Having found each dog's faults during the individual examination, study of the silhouettes helps the judge to make a final decision. This is the final opportunity to show off the best attributes of your dog. The judge's choice at this point may be narrowed down to just a few specimens.

There are a number of faults listed in the Standard. The judge must, at times, weigh one fault against another, giving particular attention to those faults that are known to be hereditary. Although the Standard specifies two points of

Candace McLaughton and Ch. Kleingaul's Spit Shine won Best Junior Handler at the 1991 SCA National Specialty.   *Booth*

disqualification, the judge is also governed by the rules of the American Kennel Club, some of which call for disqualification under certain circumstances for all breeds. A judge has no choice in this matter and may sometimes have to disqualify a seemingly excellent specimen.

Most judges agree that the cardinal virtues of a show dog, regardless of breed, are soundness, condition, balance, and type. Although there is considerable difference of opinion as to the relative importance of each, the final decision is always influenced by those four considerations. The first two are readily determined for all breeds, but balance and type are considerably influenced by the Standard of the breed being judged.

Frequently exhibitors, especially novices, have difficulty in understanding why a judge puts their dog up at one show but fails to place it a few weeks later. There are two good reasons for this. First, the competition may be of different quality. Secondly, dogs, like all living animals, change from time to time. The change may be gradual and not immediately noticed by the owner. This is particularly true of Schipperkes when condition of coat and alertness in the ring count heavily.

The judge is limited to an average of two minutes per dog in the ring. The dogs are placed as the judge sees them that day. A judge cannot speculate on future development nor attempt to remember past performance. The past record of any dog should have no bearing on the decision. This is all the more reason why the judge should be certain that all placings are governed by the Standard, regardless of who is at the other end of the lead. To do otherwise would be a disservice to exhibitors, as well as to any breed.

12

The Schipperke
in Obedience

SCHIPPERKES are eager to please and quick to learn new ideas when introduced by their owners. But because they are Schipperkes, and by nature independent and curious dogs, many owners find it beneficial to pursue Obedience training.

The most valuable part of training is the understanding and companionship that develops between dog and owner. A properly trained Schipperke will learn to Come when called, to Stay on command, and to Heel in an orderly manner beside the owner. This basic training makes life much easier in many ways. Should the house door, the car door, the kennel or the crate open unexpectedly, or the dog has wandered away, the owner can be relaxed and confident that a command to Stay or Come will be obeyed. A trained dog is a happier dog—knowing what is expected and able to cope with new situations.

Obedience training is the easiest and surest method to attain this end. Class work with a reputable trainer will start both dog and handler correctly. Whether or not they decide to compete in an Obedience Trial can be evaluated after the training course is completed.

Obedience Trials are proof of the ability of a dog and handler to work together performing certain exercises at each skill level. After the dog has demonstrated a thorough knowledge of the basic commands, of Heel, Sit, Stay and Come, they may progress to more advanced work with dumbbells, jumps, and scent work. Dogs can earn degrees including C.D. (Companion Dog), C.D.X.

Am/Can Ch. Hovde's Hi-Hat Jim Dandy Am/Can UD—the first Schipperke to finish a championship and Utility title in both Canada and the United States. He finished his Canadian Championship and his CDX on the same day. *Mikron*

(Companion Dog Excellent), U.D. (Utility Dog), T.D. (Tracking Dog), T.D.X. (Tracking Dog Excellent), and the highest title of distinction OTCh. (Obedience Trial Champion). Obedience Trials are held separately or in conjunction with a dog show. Numerous Schipperkes have titles in both Conformation and Obedience.

OBEDIENCE TRIALS IN THE UNITED STATES

In the early 1930s The American Kennel Club granted tentative approval for recognition and acceptance of obedience tests similar to trials held in England. Prior to 1936, AKC permitted a few clubs to try out the British rules and test feasibility and American acceptance. This tentative approval included rules, standards, and the awarding of titles or degrees. The first regulations and standards for Obedience Test Trials were adopted on March 10, 1936, then completely revised seven months later on November 10, 1936.

Von Vozz Mr. Goodbar, UD demonstrates the **Heel Free**, a basic exercise required to earn the Companion Dog (CD) title.

Following AKC's formal adoption of the Obedience standards, the Westchester Kennel Club held a licensed trial in September of 1936. Eighteen dogs entered in Novice and Open and were judged by Helene Whitehouse Walker. Thereafter, the obedience test movement gained unexpected and unprecedented momentum. Helene Whitehouse Walker was elected president of the Obedience Test Club and was a driving force in promoting Obedience Trials. She and her kennel manager, Blanche Saunders, trekked across America from coast to coast in a trailer with three Poodles, entering trials, giving exhibitions, and answering eager questions which had poured into headquarters at Bedford Hills, New York.

In September 1937, the Obedience Test Club held a Specialty at Rye, New York. The magazine, *Harpers Bazaar*, November 1937, reported the events at this Specialty intensively and concluded that "it had become an accepted fact that Obedience was an all-breed proposition." Among the sixty-two entrants was a Schipperke, Ch. Michael Son of Ti, owned by Howard Classen, who attracted interest because Schipperkes were not associated with training.

The growing pains of Obedience were marked by confusion and misunderstanding among contestants, trainers, and judges as to how the rules and standards were to be interpreted. Judges were few and their ideas of scoring were attuned

When the handler stops, the Schipperke must sit promptly at the handler's side.

largely to local practices. This was confusing and frustrating to enthusiasts who were courageous enough to show to an out-of-state judge. An example of these difficulties is reflected in *The American Kennel Gazette*, November 1937 issue, which stated: "[The dog]'s failure to qualify was largely due to technicalities. New York judges faulted the Boston people because of differences in training routine. Boston people have been taught About Turn means *left* about. New Yorkers say "Wrong, it means *right* about." A trivial matter? Not at all, because these minor differences accumulated throughout the separate parts of the tests and meant important swings in final scores and placings.

As obedience tests grew in national stature, competition became intense and performance of some individual dogs began to hit the perfect or near-perfect limits, then competency and uniformity of scoring became the rule rather than the exception.

The initiation of Obedience competition into dog shows opened a new era for the Schipperke breed. Particularly adapted and receptive, the Schipperke found a new level of accomplishments.

Von Vozz Mr. Goodbar, UD clears the **Bar Jump** with ease.

Von Vozz Mr. Goodbar, UD demonstrates the **Retrieve Over the High Jump**, an exercise for a Companion Dog Excellent (CDX) title.

SCHIPPERKES IN OBEDIENCE—1930s

The accomplishments of Schipperkes and their handlers is organized in this chapter according to the decade of activity under the name of the owner. This is by no means a list of every person who has handled a Schipperke to an Obedience title. Rather, it is a list compiled from the records of the Schipperke Club of America, Inc., of owner and/or handlers of Schipperkes who have advanced the Schipperke breed in Obedience.

HOWARD CLAUSSEN owned one of the first Schipperkes to achieve success in the early days of Obedience. He was Ch. Michael Son of Ti, CDX. This Schipperke was the first of the breed to win titles and achieve top placings against the best Obedience dogs in the country. The press confirmed his outstanding ring work in headlines of some Eastern newspapers: "Obedience Test Goes to Schipperke—1st in Field of Twenty-Two" "Schipperke Is Best in Obedience Test—First in Utility" "Mike—Most Consistent Dog in Obedience World." "Micky" had passed two out of the three required legs in Utility when he died unexpectedly.

Mr. Claussen's second Schipperke, Ch. Ti-De Son of Ti, CDX, gained his champion title in three quick five-point shows. He won ten placings out of twelve times shown.

1940 TO 1950

GENE HARRINGTON from Indiana owned a Schipperke credited with being the second Schipperke in the United States to win an Obedience degree. This dog, Captain Dandy of Jet-O, earned a Companion Dog (CD) degree in 1940.

Shadrach, another Schipperke owned and handled by Mr. Harrington, had the honor of earning the second Schipperke Utility degree to be awarded in the United States. Shadrach earned the UD degree in 1946 but lost the opportunity to be the first Schipperke to earn the UD degree because early obedience rules included passing a tracking test as a part of the degree. Because of this regulation, after completing the other requirements for Utility, Shadrach had to wait eleven months to compete in the tracking test.

KATHARINE LANE, a Boston artist-sculptor, was among the first Schipperke owners in New England to participate as a bench show and Obedience exhibitor. Her Schipperke, Poulette of Kelso, won her CDX on September 10, 1942. Katharine Lane later became an Obedience judge.

INEZ MANWARING from New England showed Suzette of Kelso II to her CD in 1947. In 1948, Suzette earned a near perfect score of 199 out of 200 points and a Highest Scoring Dog in Trial enroute to completing her CDX. She continued her winning record and acquired the Utility degree in 1948.

MRS. FRANK MILLER—Ch. La Belle of Mrs. Miller's Franswold

In 1946, Shadrach, UD earned the second Utility degree to be awarded to a Schipperke in the United States. Early Obedience rules included passing a tracking test after completing the requirements of a UD before the title was awarded.

Kennels in Portland, Oregon, earned her CD degree in 1941, making this Schipperke the first dual-titled Schipperke on the West Coast.

L. FLOYD NEWLIN, an Indianapolis area resident, owned a Schipperke of note in the mid-1940s named Ch. Spooks of Jet-O, UD. Spooks won his CD and CDX degrees in 1946 and his UD in 1948. He was shown successfully in the conformation ring as well, making him a versatile and outstanding representative of the breed.

KATHERINE WELLMAN—was another ''Bostonian'' who earned high places in Obedience during this decade. She was president of the New England Dog Training Club, Inc., which was the first Obedience club to incorporate and to become a member club of the American Kennel Club. Although Ms. Wellman began with a German Shepherd Dog, she ultimately went over completely to Schipperkes. Prior to her untimely accidental death while horseback riding in 1955, she had acquired Menelik of Kelso and other Schipperkes to round out her kennel. Menelik earned his Companion Dog Excellent (CDX) title and was one of the three dogs who passed the tracking test.

L. H. WINSTON—was active in the early 1940s with her Schipperke, Ch. Lady's Laddie Boy, who earned the CDX title and UD (which in those days required that the dog also pass a tracking test). Thus, he became the first of the breed to go to the very top.

A Schipperke of note in the mid-1940s was Ch. Spooks of Jet-O, UD, owned by L. Floyd Newlin. Spooks won his CD and CDX degrees in 1946 and his UD in 1948.

168

1950 THROUGH EARLY 1960s

The 1950s and 1960s saw a general increase in Obedience activities in the United States, and numerous degrees were awarded.

HORACE CARR of Ohio owned, trained and handled Ch. Jingo of Beaumont, UD, who had a brilliant career. Jingo earned a CD degree in 1948 with three High in Trial awards, a remarkable record. He earned the CDX degree in 1948 and the UD in 1949. As the only dual titleholder in the Midwest, he drew a great deal of attention to the breed. Mr. Carr later acquired Beaumont's Nicodemus, who earned a CDX in 1954.

ALFRED J. COMSTOCK of Michigan (said to be a nephew of Walter Comstock the first Schipperke importer in the United States) trained Captain of Northridge to a UD degree in 1955. Captain was an enthusiastic performer in the ring and placed in the ribbons many times.

MR. and MRS. LLOYD EVANS from the St. Louis area owned Ch. Marless Beau Brummel, UD. Beau Brummel earned his CD in 1957, CDX in 1958, and UD degree in 1960. He was a consistently high scorer and outstanding performer. Beau Brummel was trained in Open and Utility work at home with instructions learned from an Obedience book with no formal class attendance.

G. ELLYSON owned Ch. Rockhound of Rose Glen who attained a UD degree in 1960, becoming another Western dual titlist.

N. FOWLER from the San Francisco-Oakland area took two Schipperkes through to UD degrees. Ajax of Rose Glen earned a UD degree in 1953 and Normadel Starlight Ambie finished to UD in 1955. Both Schipperkes had high scores with Ambie earning a tie for Highest Scoring Dog in Trial.

H. E. HOPKINS and her daughter, Elaine, trained several Schipperkes in the 1950s. Their first Schipperke shown in Obedience trials was Diamond Hill Alka. She won a CD in 1948 and a CDX in 1950 with high scores. Another one of their Schipperkes, Alka's Ebony Jewel, earned a CD in 1951. Then, after earning the first score toward a CDX in 1951, this bitch had to have a front leg amputated at the shoulder after a fight with a large dog. Despite this serious handicap, she finished her CDX degree on three legs and heart, with scores of 199 and 199½!

MR. and MRS. CARLTON JONES May-He-Co Kennels, were leaders in Obedience training and competition in the 1950s. Outstanding among May-He-Co dual title holders were Ch. May-He-Co's Lin-Breeze, CDX (1955), Ch. Ima Brat of Jet-O, CDX (1956), Ch. May-He-Co's Don Im-Ree-Kardu, CDX (winner of class First), Ch. May-He-Co's Dan Dee Daun, CD (1959). Other CDX holders were May-He-Co's Lin Reinita, CDX (1953), May-He-Co's Lin-Bingo, CDX (1955), May-He-Co's Dona Territa, CDX (1958) and May-He-Co's Don Ricardo VIII, CDX (1965).

Other outstanding May-He-Co Schipperkes owned, trained and shown by other owners were May-He-Co's Dona Merito, CDX (1954) and May-He-Co's Pan-Dee Tawn, CDX (1960), owned by Mr. and Mrs. R. W. Gellatly of River-

This Schipperke is retrieving a glove, an exercise for a Utility Dog (UD).

A Schipperke locating a scent article in this Utility exercise.

170

side, California. V. A. Buffenbarger earned CDX on May-He-Co's To Jette in 1960. Another Buffenbarger Schipperke, May-He-Co's Tinker Belle attained UD in 1964.

MR. and MRS. R. T. KERCHIEL of Minnesota actively trained and exhibited in the mid-1950s. Their first Schipperke was Von Kay's Fascinatin' Flyer who earned the CD in 1954 and CDX in 1955. May-He-Co's Pan Des Topaz earned a CDX in 1957. Both Schipperkes won high scores while competing. A number of other Kerchiel Schipperkes were trained and shown to CD degrees.

MR. and MRS. WALTER LAKE and their daughter, Toni, of Fort Wayne, Indiana, actively participated in Obedience training and competition during the 1950s and 1960s. Ch. Toni's Tinka Tu of Beaumont, owned by Toni Lake, finished both her championship title and her UD degree in 1954. She placed numerous times in Obedience competition, and was awarded five first places and a Highest Scoring Dog in Trial in 1953. A son of Tinka Tu acquired the CDX degree in 1958, and placed in several Open classes.

MRS. RONALD MACDONALD owned Ch. Nahiman Yeoman, who was actively campaigned in the late 1950s. He finished a CD in 1956 and the CDX in 1958 with first and second placings. In 1960, another Macdonald Schipperke, Ebonette Maid, started on her remarkable career. By 1962, Ebie had earned her championship title as well as the Utility degree and Tracking titles, thereby earning the distinction of becoming the first Schipperke to attain all possible titles both in conformation and Obedience. Mrs. Macdonald later trained and finished Ch. Toni's Mark of Dark Star to a UD in 1965. In 1969 she campaigned Ch. Ebonmark's Penniworth to CD, CDX, and UD.

TONI MARTIN of St. Louis, Missouri, became interested in Obedience training and finished a CD degree on her first Schipperke, Twinkle Toes of Valley View, in 1954. She later became an Obedience instructor and a professional handler both in conformation and Obedience. After her marriage to John Strasburger she continued training and exhibiting, earning a CD degree on their jointly owned Best in Show winner Ch. Ye Ole Lamplighter of San Dil, CD.

EARL TUCKER owned the Highest scoring Schipperke on the West Coast in 1954, Barlan Dixie CDX. This Schipperke placed in the ribbons for nearly every leg of her degrees and twice received a perfect score of 200 to win Highest Scoring Dog in Trial.

OLIVE MILLER of Phoenix, Arizona, became interested in Obedience training and competition. Her Ch. Sun Valley's Adobe Lad became an early Western dual titleholder, earning a CD degree in 1954, a CDX in 1955, and a UD in 1957. Adobe Lad placed in the ribbons consistently with five class Firsts. Sun Valley's Rebaba Reba earned CD degree in 1959 and CDX in 1961 with high scores and class Firsts. Another Miller Schipperke, Sun Valley's Kiva Kachina earned a CDX in 1964.

An outstanding record was made when Best in Show winner Ch. Pine Hill's Indigo Bill attained a CD degree in 1960 making Bill the first Best in Show winner to earn an Obedience degree.

Ch. Hobbiton's Tinuvial of L.C., CDX.

MARTHA TATUM began to exhibit Lo-Lane Cindy late in 1958. Cindy earned a CD in 1958, a CDX in 1959, and a UD in 1961. She placed often in the classes with several Highest Scoring Dog in Trial awards. This little Schipperke earned a great deal of admiration for the breed through her performances and earned a perfect 200 score in 1963 to climax an impressive career.

BETTY THOMPSON of Tulsa, Oklahoma, owned Farskane Inky who finished CDX in 1953 and UD in 1955 placing often in obedience classes. In 1955 she won Highest Scoring Dog in Trial. Another Thompson dog, Farskane Cinders completed CD degree in 1957, CDX in 1958, and UD in 1960, placing often in the ribbons.

FLORENCE TRESEDER (Country Kennels) trained numerous Schipperkes to advance obedience degrees. Although Ch. May-He-Co's Ecloo's Madame Velvet obtained her CD and CDX degrees under the ownership of Mr. Jones, she was trained by and earned her UD degree (1955) under Miss Treseder's ownership. May-He-Co's Don Pio Pico, jointly owned by Florence Treseder and Mrs. Jones, also earned all Obedience degrees, CD and CDX in 1954 and UD in 1955.

Ch. Black Angel's Casey, UD.

MR. and MRS. D. ALLEN of Tennessee purchased Hanouk De La Mottelette from France. He was imported to this country in the late 1950s. Hanouk was sired by the noted French champion, Ch. Aurick du Bord des Etangs, a Best in Show Schipperke in Belgium, in 1955. Hanouk earned a CD degree in 1960 and a CDX in 1962. The Allens competed actively in the Obedience ring throughout the 1960s, earning degrees on many Schipperkes. An outstanding performer during that period was Jadel's Petite D'Or who earned CD in 1962, CDX in 1963, and UD in 1964 with high scores. D'Or placed often in the ribbons with some Highest Scoring Dog awards. Other Allen winners were Topwatch Aye Aye who earned UD in 1966, Topwatch Armada, CDX, (later owned by L. and E. Hay), a Highest Scoring Dog in Trial Schipperke, and French Champion Huchette Des Lutins Noirs, CDX, in 1964.

REV. ALFRED BACKUS of Indianapolis acquired CD degrees on some Schipperkes in the 1940s and continued Obedience activities into the 1960s. He earned a CD on Pixy of Nelfred in 1959, CDX in 1961, and UD in 1962.

THE SIXTIES TO THE NINETIES

The 1960s continued an escalated interest in obedience activities. The emergence of an outstanding star in the Obedience field heralded a new era for the Schipperke breed.

MAJOR and MRS. DEAN ALLEN continued to be active Obedience participants in the 1970s. Initially from Tennessee, they later moved to Alaska. A number of their Schipperkes, bearing the Topwatch prefix, obtained Obedience degrees. Their Topwatch Hero, UD, averaged 194 in Open and Utility work. Their bloodlines included some imports and some non-black specimens.

JOAN ASMUSSIN of Florida owned and trained OTCh. Sable Little Lulu, UD. Lulu earned an average score of 194 and was the second Schipperke to earn an Obedience trial Champion title.

LOIS BORDER of Oregon trained Cracker Jack deBorder to a CD in 1969. He completed the last CDX leg July 7, 1974. He earned his Canadian Am CD in May 1973. Am/Can Ch. Roetmop Captain Coalby earned his Am CD in February 1973. Ch. Char Coalette Dixie Cup, CD, earned an average of 193.5 for her CD.

O.T. Ch. Sable Little Lulu, UD, owned by Joan Asmussen of Florida earned an average score of 194 and was the second Schipperke to earn an Obedience Trial Champion title. "Lulu" is on the right, posing with Dream On's Ebony Doll, CD.

Ch. Char Coalette Dixie Cup, CD, owned by Lois Border, earned an average score of 193.5 for her Companion Dog title.

GLORIA BLATT owned and handled Ebon Imp Star of Kismet, UD. This Schipperke earned average scores of 195 for a three year period, and won Highest Scoring Dog in Trial and several first places. Gloria Blatt is also an Obedience judge.

WILMA DAME owned one of the most outstanding winners in Obedience in the 1970s: Wil-Cle Joc Ann de Noirmont, Am/Can UD. Called "Kriket," this great worker was top Obedience Schipperke for 1971 and 1973. She won multiple Highest Scoring Dog in Trial awards. In addition to her outstanding record in the United States, Kriket also placed in Obedience competition in Canada. At one trial in which she was entered, Kriket proved her intelligence. She was in the Utility ring going for the Bar Jump, when she misjudged the takeoff by a step. In mid-air Kriket felt herself about to fall on the bar. No doubt her brain was clicking as fast as her body was moving. Much to the astonishment

175

Wil-Cle Joc Ann de Noirmont, UD—The SCA Top Obedience Schipperke in 1971 and 1973 and winner of multiple Highest Scoring Dog in Trial awards.

of everyone present she gave a twist which carried her over. She won a score of 199½ that day, earning the distinction of High Scoring Dog in Trial.

Other Schipperkes owned by Mrs. Dame during the 1970s include Wil-Cle Freddy's Freeloader, CDX, Wil-Cle Velvet Pepper, CDX, and Wil-Cle Skipper, CD.

Wil-Cle Bubbles of Dancer, Am/Can UD, daughter of Joc Ann Noirmont, started a long, successful Obedience career that spanned eight years. She stayed active into the mid-1980s, earning an average of 194 with several Highest Scoring Dog in Trial awards and was the SCA Top Winning Obedience Schipperke in 1980, 1981, 1982, and 1983. Bubbles, along with her kennel mate, Wil-Cle's Angelic Devil, Am/Can UD, were shown in the Obedience Brace class, often placing first. Mrs. Dame also owned another good working Schipperke in Wil-Cle Pride of Gem who averaged 196 while gaining her CD.

GALE AND PAULA ENSIGN of California owned Ch. Skipalong's Ossa Boy, CDX, who earned scores averaging 195 with many placings and a High Scoring Dog in Trial.

LISA FAULKNER of Oregon owned Inkprint of Jet-O, UD, who was the SCA Top Obedience Schipperke in 1972. Ms. Faulkner's Terrilas Travelin Gypsy, CD, won Highest Scoring Dog in Trial and two other class placings in gaining the Novice title in the 1970s.

TINA FAY of Texas owned Hobbiton's One of the Nine, CD, who began his Obedience career in 1988. The SCA National Specialty that year saw One of the Nine win High Scoring Dog in Trial.

CATHRYN FLISZAR of Missouri owned a champion Schipperke, Ch. A.R.E.S. Magnum Man, UD, who won numerous High Scoring Dog in Trial

Wil-Cle Bubbles of Dancer, Am/Can UD, won several Highest Scoring Dog in Trial awards and many class placings. She was the SCA Top Obedience Schipperke in 1980, 1982, 1982, and 1983.

Wil-Cle Bubbles of Dancer, Am/Can UD (left) and Wil-Cle Angelic Devil, Am/Can UD (right) model their Obedience awards.

and class placings. He had a four year average of 195 and was the SCA Top Obedience Schipperke in 1984. A.R.E.S. Don Duts, CDX, was also an outstanding obedience Schipperke. He had average scores of 195 through Novice and Open with many class placings.

KATHY FRIEDT'S Belique Kennels made its appearance in 1969. During the 1970's, Schipperkes from this kennel were active both in Obedience and conformation. Ms. Freidt's first Schipperke was Spock's Vulcan O'Dex. Her Am/Can Ch. Roetmop Captain Caius was awarded the CD degree in 1973. In February, 1974, he earned a CDX. Roetmop Elf completed CD in three consecutive shows with scores of 189, 193, and 193.

BOBBIE GAVIN of Virginia owned an outstanding obedience Schipperke in the late 1970s; OTCh. Gra-Bars Dancing Duchess. This bitch was the first Schipperke to win the title of Obedience Trial Champion (OTCh.). Her Obedience career was outstanding, and she earned numerous Highest Scoring Dog in Trial awards, including the 1977 Eastern Regional Division of the Gaines Super Dog competition. She was the Top Obedience Schipperke for the years 1976, 1977, 1978, and 1979 and averaged scores of 196 over four years of work. She would have undoubtedly achieved many more excellent scores had it not been for the untimely death of her owner.

MR. and MRS. JACK GRIGGS purchased Holiday from a Tacoma, Washington, kennel in 1960. She started her training with the Philadelphia Training Club in 1962 and earned CD, CDX, and UD degrees all within an 8½

Wil-Cle Pride of Gem, Am/Can UD averaged 196 while gaining her Companion Dog (CD) title.

Inkprint of Jet-O, UD—top winning Obedience Schipperke for 1971.

month period. A truly remarkable record! After the Griggs moved to the Chicago area, Holiday was campaigned extensively. She had eighty-seven class Firsts with *thirty-three* Highest Scoring Dog in Trial awards. Her qualifying score lifetime show average for 177 classes was 197.5. Holiday had nine consecutive Highest Scoring Dog in Trial and *four perfect scores* of 200. Holiday has also passed the TD (Tracking test) three times. The tremendous performance of this Schipperke won many compliments for the breed. She earned the honor of being listed in *Popular Dogs* magazine as one of the Top Obedience Dogs of the Past and was retired from competition in 1968.

The Griggs earned Obedience degrees on numerous other Schipperkes during the 1960s. Outstanding were Gem Jet's Jody who earned CD degree in 1961, CDX in 1962, and UD in 1963. Jody won many Highest Scoring Dog in Trial awards also establishing an impressive record. Ch. Vibra's Image of Jet-O earned CD in 1963, CDX in 1964, and UD in 1966. Another Griggs' Schipperke, Ch. Skipalong's Glade, attained a TD title in 1970. Their consistently high standard of performance proved that excellent training and the intelligence of the breed can produce a winning combination.

L. HANSEN of Colorado owned Ch. Valkyra Dauphine O'Happy Glen, CDX, who earned average scores of 195 and all first placings while gaining the CDX title.

C. HARMON—Warlock's Little Dream Weaver, CD, owned by C. Harmon of Alaska, average 194.5 with Highest Scoring Dog in Trial. This dog placed in every Trial, winning three firsts and a fourth.

DAWN HRIBAR—Skipalong's Cindy Roo, Am/Can CDX, placed six

Holiday, UDT and Jem-Jet's Jody won multiple Best Obedience Brace in Show awards.

out of the seven times shown, winning an American and Canadian Specialty Highest Scoring Dog in Trial plus an all-breed Highest Scoring Dog in Trial.

D. IVERSON owned an outstanding Wyoming Schipperke, Ch. Odex's Cosmet Laser Beam, CD, co-owned by L. Snell, who averaged 195 with two High Scoring Dog in Trial awards, and a first and second in five shows.

KAREN AND PATRICK JOHNSON owned Ch. Von Kay's Whiz Bang who did exceptionally well in both obedience and conformation in the early 1970's. "Whizzer" obtained a CD in 1970 with scores of 198, 199, and 197½. In 1971, scores of 198, 195, and 198 earned him the CDX. He was also given the Dog World Award for obtaining the degrees in three consecutive trials. He earned at least two High Scoring Dog in Trial with scores of 199 and 197½.

JANET KUNKLE of Oregon owned, trained and handled Ch. Beligue's Glory Seeker, UDT, a good example of Schipperke versatility. At one show, this bitch won a Group Third and Highest Scoring Dog in Trial!

VICKI MAHER showed an exceptional dog during the 1980s, Ch. Belique's AWOL From Ni-Kel, CDX. Vicki and AWOL won two first places, one third and one fourth place in gaining his CD title. AWOL is also an all-breed Best in Show winner.

Skipalong's Cindy Roo, Am/Can CDX, won an American and a Canadian Specialty Highest Scoring Dog in Trial as well as an all-breed Highest Scoring Dog in Trial.

KATHRYN MARSHALL'S Mar's Lil Skipper Kay, UD, had high scores throughout his Obedience career. He finished the CD (1964), the CDX (1965), and the UD (1967) with many Highest Scoring Dog in Trial awards.

SHARON MCKAY owned Ch. Landmark's Damon of Hi-Line, UD, who averaged 192.5 while gaining his titles.

BOBBIE MEYERS became interested in the breed and purchased Wilbet's Ursa Minor. Ch. Wilbet's Ursa Minor, UD, earned average scores of 193.5 and was the SCA Top Winning Obedience Schipperke in 1975.

KATHY MONTGOMERY has bred, owned and handled several Schipperkes to Obedience titles, and is the breeder of Kleingaul's Sara Lee, CDX, the SCA's Top Obedience Schipperke of 1990 and the breeder and co-owner of Ch. Kleingaul's Spitfire O'Freewood, CDX.

MARY MONROE of Texas, owned Jetstar's Mary Poppins, UD, who earned an average score of 195 over three years of showing and placed many times in the classes. Another outstanding Monroe Schipperke was Tanya De Tarter, CDX, co-owned by M. Monroe and M. Tarter. This Schipperke earned average scores of 195.

J. PABST was active in 1989 when California was the site of the SCA

Ch. Tudox Beautiful Dreamer, CDX, enthusiastically executes the **Retrieve Over the High Jump**.

National Specialty. Three Schipperkes tied for Highest Scoring Dog in Trial with the same score of 196; Kleingaul's Spitfire O'Freewood (later a Champion) owned by J. Pabst and K. Montgomery, Warlock's Little Dream Weaver, CDX, owned by C. Harmon, and Wil-Cle Pride of Gem, UD, owned by W. Dame, After two run-offs, Pride emerged the winner.

DR. SHIRLEY QUILLEN of Ohio who, during 1990, handled her Schipperkes to a Championship, a CD, a CDX, and a UD. This is truly a remarkable feat. One of her Schipperkes is Ch. Tudox Beautiful Dreamer, CDX.

C. RANDEL owned Kleingaul's Sara Lee, CDX, who was first in the classes nine times, second twice, and third once. Moving into Open work, she continued the same great scoring with three first places, one second, one third, and one fourth in Open A. She was the SCA Top Obedience Schipperke in 1990.

RUTH ROSSBACH—Ch. E'Lans Yentl, Am/Can CDX, owned by Ruth Rossbach from New Jersey was the SCA Top Winning Schipperke in 1987.

GORDON SOMMER of Oregon owned the top Obedience Schip for 1970, Ch. Graham Cracker of Jet-O, CDX.

K. THOMPSON owned and trained Morning Glory's Pepper Roni, UD.

182

This Schipperke averaged scores of 194 and earned several Highest Scoring Dog in Trial awards.

DONNA WALTON—Another outstanding Obedience Schipperke was Ch. Wilbet's Merry Mistletoe, UD. She was also the dam of an all champion litter including Ch. Do-Well's Nitro, a Best in Show winner.

MEDA WHITLEY—started a great working Schipperke named Dr. H. C. Burns, UD, on a terrific Obedience career in the late 1970s earning a perfect score of 200 points in his second try for CD. In nearly four years of showing, he averaged 195.5 with four High Scoring Dog in Trial awards, and many class placings. The Schipperke Club of America held its first Obedience Trial in connection with National Specialty in 1980. Dr. H. C. Burns was High Scoring Dog at this trial.

KYLIE JO WOLKENHEIM was a Jr. Handler in the Obedience ring with a nice working Schipperke, Harmony's Devil Dust Flash. This dog earned his U-CD with class placements, his Canadian CD with class placements and his American CD with one first place, two seconds, one third, and two fourth, all in the same year. His owner/handler was eleven years old. Flash continued his winning ways, earning his U-CDX and his Canadian CDX. He placed in all Trials while gaining his CDXs.

D. WOLVERTON of Louisiana owned Turras Geraldine, UD, later owned by Mrs. D. Wood. This bitch averaged 192.5 while earning her titles over four years of work.

E. YAMASKI owned Eds Juu Ipo, CDX. This dog averaged scores of

U-CDX Harmony's Devil Dust Flash, Am/Can CDX.

198 through Novice and Open work and placed first or second for each leg of each title plus a Highest Scoring Dog in Trial from Open.

LOOKING TO THE FUTURE

In 1990, Ch. A.R.E.S. Celebrity MD, CD, was in the top spot followed closely by Ch. Belique's AWOL From Ni-Kel, CDX, owned by V. Maher and Ch. Blackjacks Majestk Onyx, CDX, owned by L. Sims and Delfino. Ch. Charr Coalette Dixie Cup, UD, owned by L. Border from Oregon, won her Utility title in 1990, with two first places and one second place. As the year progressed, Celebrity was still on top with A.R.E.S. St. Nicholas, CDX, in second place.

At this time, six Champions were in the ratings. By fall, Kleingaul's Sara Lee, CDX, was earning scores which boosted her into second place and was the eventual Top Winning Schipperke in Obedience. Other Schipperkes' names began to appear, including Learjet's Black Irish Lass, CDX, owned by M. Brinkley. This Schipperke had a High Scoring Dog in Trial while gaining her CDX.

In summarizing the years since the beginning of Obedience in this country, there are many examples of capable trainers and receptive, intelligent Schip-

Kleingaul's Sara Lee, UD—SCA Top Winning Obedience Schipperke for 1990.

184

perkes. There are many UD Schipperkes who are also Champions of record. This list grows longer each year. Now Tracking Dog titles are appearing more frequently. The success of so many Schipperkes in the Obedience ring proves the native intelligence of the breed is being maintained by breeders. Obedience work with Schipperkes can be a satisfying experience for all fanciers. Even if the Schipperke owner is not interested in conformation or Obedience competition, training can be rewarding. A well-trained Schipperke is always a joy.

Roy C. Henre, owner of the famed Jet-O kennels, finishing his 100th champion, Ch. Black Rambo of Jet-O, in 1975. *Ludwig*

13

The Art of
Breeding Schipperkes

T HERE ARE MANY theories on breeding. One method popular among novices is to breed a bitch to a dog that has won the most Best of Breeds for the year or sired the most champions last year, without regard to whether or not the stud is suited for the bitch. This chapter is presented to discuss several theories regarding the breeding of animals. It is not a complete discourse on genetics, and successful theories used by many kennels may not be covered. It is hoped, however, that veteran and novice breeders will both benefit from the knowledge and experience shared here.

CONTINUING THE LINE

There are many theories of genetics which may explain why breeding certain animals results in excellent specimens of the breed. Many breeders try to reproduce great dogs of the past by duplicating as closely as possible the combination that produced a great dog or bitch. This might be accomplished by breeding the son of a great stud dog to the daughter of a bitch who previously whelped a champion out of that great stud.

For example, to reproduce the bloodline of Ch. Maroufke of Kelso, a male descendant of Maroufke or his sire, Ch. Marouf of Kelso, might be bred to a bitch descended from Maroufke's maternal grandsire, Ch. 'Ti Noir of Kelso, or to a direct female descendant, such as Ch. Arlette of Kelso or her dam, Ch. Dolette of Kelso.

Many breeders believe that good combinations sometimes strike again. Many lines and families, when bred to another line, produce exceptional results. It is safe to say that any good combination which has produced several good specimens is a good fit. Successful combinations may also be accomplished by breeding a dog of one line to all bitches of the same family.

KORTHALS' THEORY

In the year 1870, a man named Korthals, the son of a wealthy Flemish farmer, was determined to breed a superior wire-haired hunting dog. He selected twelve dogs and bitches. None of these specimans was purebred in the sense we know it today. All were excellent hunting dogs and each had a quality Mr. Korthals admired. He bred litters from these dogs and selected the best offspring of each. Next, he inbred the best dog and bitch, that is, he bred these closely related offspring to each other. After inbreeding for several generations, he found it necessary to outcross to other pure inbred strains he had developed. However, each of these strains was unrelated to the other strains. He then selected and inbred the resulting best from each mating.

Korthals' breeding system was as follows:

- Select the best specimens
- Outcross
- Select the best offspring of outcrossing
  and
- Inbreed the best specimens

This system can be carried on almost indefinitely without fear of poor results. Of course, this man was quite ruthless in culling his breeding stock, and he bred only about 10 percent of all the stock he produced. However, it was by this system that his breed, the Wire-haired Pointing Griffon, was first developed.

THE LOWE THEORY—THE FEMALE LINE

In the early 1890s, an Australian named Bruce Lowe wrote a book outlining a theory for breeding good specimens. Not only was he a student of pedigrees and a mathematician, he was also one of the earliest disciples of the theory of female dominance, believing that all great sires were the result of breeding to strong female lines. Mr. Lowe further believed all good sires were the result of inbreeding to female families which had produced exceptional sires.

His theories can be applied to Schipperke breeding by listing all known champions dating from 1930 to the present. Some energetic statistician, armed with computer, calculator, and a complete set of stud books dating back to 1925, would need to trace all the female ancestors as far back as the 1925 Stud Book. The bitches would then be grouped in families, and the bitch listed in the 1925 Stud Book with the most champion descendants would be designated as the "number one" taproot bitch. The next highest number of champions would be designated as the "number two" taproot bitch and so forth until all the champions are listed in their proper family. Thereafter, by studying the above statistics, it would be possible to analyze the results and determine which families produced the best sires. Each year it would be possible to compile, from the list of champions, the leading families according to champions produced.

This system has its drawbacks as it is dependent on the efforts made to finish each champion as well as on the personal circumstances of each breeder or owner. As proof that this theory is used to some extent by many breeders, Mr. Lowe pointed out that these breeders, if given a choice of two bitches of equal quality, pick the bitch with the best production record.

THE DOSAGE SYSTEM

A Frenchman named Col. Vuillier devised a system he called the Dosage System. He reasoned that all great purebred animals had something in common which made them stand out over the mediocre ones. His system entailed laborious research in pedigrees. To apply his theory to Schipperkes, it would be necessary to trace all the excellent champions for a period of years and assign them points for their location in the pedigree. Most of the great dogs should have had a high percentage of their ancestry from only about twenty or so dogs and bitches after nine generations. Col Vuillier assigned eight points in the 9th generation, sixteen points in the 8th generation, thirty-two points in the 7th generation, sixty-four in the 6th, etc., and tried to establish a norm for the percentage of bloodline necessary to produce the outstanding individual. The Dosage System would enable a breeder to reestablish bloodlines to conform with the average for the outstanding specimens of the breed.

GENETIC POTENTIAL

The real secret in breeding any two dogs is knowing the genetic possibilities of the two individuals. Marks of distinction in any kennel, or strain, are the "dominant" traits. A sire or dam that is capable of transmitting outstanding traits to many puppies is called "prepotent." A dominant trait will not change and become recessive.

In linebreeding, which relies on families, but not the breeding of very close relatives, dominant genes are greatly magnified. With inbreeding, such as mother and son, every gene good and bad is enormously intensified. Inbreeding two specimens of sound, stable, linebred backgrounds who are of excellent quality themselves can bring exciting results. However, two dogs of questionable quality or from outcrossed and unrelated backgrounds (even though they are mother/ son) have many more unknown genetic possibilities that will be redoubled and brought to the surface. The results could be disastrous from a breeder's viewpoint. The old rule of thumb, "Like begets Like," holds true no matter what the relationship. Breeders should also remember that **each parent contributes 50 percent of the genes**.

Breeders should consider the opportunity to use brothers and sisters of famous champions and producers. A brother or sister to a great dog will carry a very close genetic makeup to the great one. Sometimes, a fault or injury will make a show career impossible for them. Do not disregard well-bred dogs. This is not to advocate that the breeders should not be selective. Sometimes, however, the well-bred sister or brother will produce just as good or better specimens as their famous relatives if given equal opportunity and good bitches.

John Madden, great American horse breeder, once said, "Breed the best to the best and hope for the best. In this way, you will have good years and bad years. When you produce a champion, the theorist will then tell you how it happened."

14

The Schipperke Bitch and Her Litter

As WITH OTHER breeds, the estrous cycle (heat season) of the Schipperke occurs approximately every six months, although it is not unusual for some Schipperkes to experience a longer cycle. The onset of estrus may not be obvious. Some bitches exhibit symptoms so slight that the novice may miss them. The proper day to breed cannot be predicted accurately, as there is a wide variation with individuals dogs. It is better to ship the dog too early than too late.

Bitches should not be bred until they are eighteen months old or more, nor should they be bred every season after that.

PRENATAL CARE

Prior to breeding, the bitch should have a thorough veterinary examination and should be free from parasites and infection as well as being current on all booster shots, including parvovirus and rabies.

Minor problems, such as a slight dermatitis or bowel or urinary tract disturbance, which may seem insignificant in the mother, could easily be critical to a newborn puppy. The veterinarian will want to review the mother's medical history as part of a complete evaluation of her present condition and ability to bear young. In addition, any available knowledge of the dog's family history can be valuable.

The veterinarian may recommend several laboratory tests. Other tests may also be given, depending upon the results of the initial tests or when individual problems occur.

A hematocrit is a quick and simple test for anemia. The first two stages of labor require physical endurance by the mother. An anemic dog lacks normal stamina, is more apt to experience difficulties in delivering her puppies, and is more susceptible to shock, should a problem arise. Anemic bitches fatigue easily—the anemic mother may deliver part of her litter and then be unable to continue without a rest. This delay may cause stillborn puppies, retained afterbirths, and possibly result in septic metritis. Moreover, an anemic bitch is a poor surgical risk, if surgical measures are necessary to complete the delivery. Also, the anemic mother has less chance of recovery.

Because anemias are a major source of problems to pregnant animals, some veterinarians recommend that a hematocrit be repeated at two or three week intervals throughout the pregnancy even if the initial test results are within normal range.

Some veterinarians require a urine analysis be performed. The urine must be examined when fresh and should come from the first elimination in the morning. This test is important in older dogs and/or when there is an indication of increased thirst or frequency of elimination.

The stools are the best guide to the condition of the gastro-intestinal tract, and abnormalities, such as mucoid or discolored stools, should be detected and remedied early in the pregnancy. For this reason, the feces will be examined at each visit for parasites and abnormalities. Between visits, the owner should watch the bowel movements daily and report any suspected problems to the veterinarian. This should continue while the bitch is in whelp.

The veterinarian may also want to boost the bitch's distemper, parvovirus, leptospirosis, and hepatitis immunity for the pregnancy, unless she was adequately immunized within the past year. This injection not only increases the mother's immunity, but also affords initial, temporary immunity to the puppies by passing antibodies to them in the colostrum, the first milk in the breast, when they nurse.

PREGNANCY

Pregnancy is a time when the mother's body is under enormous stress. It is important that the pregnant bitch receive a well-balanced diet, but there is no need to deviate from her regular diet if it is high-quality and properly balanced. Additional foods such as cooked egg yolks and liver can help combat anemia.

Several factors influence weight gain during pregnancy, so a precise predicted gain cannot be dictated. The size of the uterus, amount of body fluids, increased size of the breasts, number and size of the puppies, and breed of the parents are all contributory elements. As a rough guide, a pregnant bitch gains approximately 15 percent of her body weight. In general, this should be the maximum. The veterinarian will make specific weight recommendations. As with their human counterparts, the weight worry in pregnant bitches lies with their gaining too much weight because obese bitches are more prone to problems at time of delivery. Knowing how much food to give a pregnant bitch can be difficult, but as a general rule of thumb, it is better to avoid overfeeding rather than underfeeding. Some breeders suggest that a maintenance diet—the calorie intake per pound of body weight should remain the same—be continued during the first month of pregnancy, then the food intake gradually increased during the remainder of gestation. At the time of whelping, the bitch may be eating 20 to 50 percent more than her normal diet.

By the seventh or eighth week of pregnancy, pressure on the stomach may reduce the amount of food the bitch can consume at one feeding. If this occurs, divide the bitch's regular meal into two or three portions and offer these smaller portions at appropriate intervals throughout the day.

If there are indications that the bitch's diet is inadequate, the veterinarian may outline further additions and corrections, including use of supplements such as vitamins, minerals, and hemantinics (compounds to combat anemia). This depends upon each individual dog's physical condition and the quality of her diet. The *veterinarian* should make the recommendations.

Allow a mother-to-be as much water as she wishes, but keep track of the amount she does drink as an approximate daily consumption. Increased water consumption might be significant, and the veterinarian will want this measured.

Milk in the diet is not necessary for lactation but may be offered in amounts to which the bitch is accustomed. *If she was not a milk drinker, there is no reason for her to become one when she is pregnant.* Many dogs cannot drink even a small amount of milk without suffering stomach upsets, and such a dog, pregnant or not, should not be given milk.

As the size of the uterus increases, the pressure on the adjacent organs may make it necessary for the pregnant bitch to urinate and defecate more frequently. This usually occurs by the eighth week of pregnancy.

A pregnant bitch *should* be encouraged to be active. While new breeders often fear that overexercise may harm the dog or cause her to abort the puppies, the reverse is true; strong abdominal muscles are needed for a normal, safe, and healthy delivery. Abundant exercise strengthens the muscles for this task. The danger lies in inadequate exercise, rather than too much. As the due date nears and the mother becomes heavy with puppies, she may begin to tire more easily. Activity should be continued, but should entail shorter and more frequent walks.

The culmination of pregnancy should occur between the 58th and 65th days. On the 58th day of gestation, the puppy is "full term," meaning it has

Ch. Dream On's Call Me Mister, Ch. Dream On's Ebony Imp, CD, and family pose for a portrait. Seven puppies in one litter is large, the average number is three or four puppies.

sufficiently matured to live outside the mother. There is no precise method available to predict the delivery date, accurately, as several factors may distort exact calculation of delivery, including the following variables:

1) conception may not have occurred for as long as 72 hours after mating,
2) large litters have a tendency toward shorter-term pregnancies,
3) the breed of dog or family within a breed may influence length of pregnancy, and
4) the endocrine system ultimately triggers the act of birth.

There are, however, a few signs to watch for which will indicate the imminent arrival of the new litter.

A check on the bitch's temperature will show a drop as much as five days ahead of whelping. It may be 100 to 99.8 degrees, a drop from the normal range of 101 to 102 degrees. The lower temperature seems to be associated with the pre-labor changes taking place within the bitch. A day or so before the whelping, the bitch will appear thinner and the hip bones will become more prominent as the weight shifts lower in the body. An internal examination at this time would likely show that the dilation of the cervix has begun.

Some veterinarians recommend an X-ray be taken of the mother at this time. X-rays reveal the number of puppies in the litter and their size, and indicate whether a normal delivery can be expected. If the puppies are too large to pass through the birth canal a Caesarean section will be performed. During the last week of pregnancy, the presence of a clear, glassy, odorless vaginal discharge is perfectly normal. Should the discharge become cloudy, discolored, or have an odor, consult your veterinarian immediately.

WHELPING

There are many variables in canine labor and delivery, so precise statements are difficult. The birth of young is easier for dogs than for their human counterparts. If a pregnant bitch is in good condition, is carrying proper weight, and possesses good muscle tone, labor is relatively effortless. However, the attitude with which a particular dog performs the whelping is highly individual.

When the bitch's temperature drops down to the 99 to 98 degree range, the initial stage of labor is imminent. Now is a good time to notify the veterinarian that assistance may be necessary within the next twenty-four hours. The vet will be prepared for a possible middle-of-the-night call, or can assist the owner in establishing contact with someone who can be reached if help is needed. Another very obvious change in the bitch's appearance will coincide with the final temperature drop. The sides of her abdomen will be tense and hard as they seemingly constrict around the uterus. Lumps can be felt at this point and these are the puppies about to be born. Once a bitch has started this final process, she will most likely refuse any food, no matter how tempting the meal. If she does eat, do not expect the food to stay down for long.

Canine labor can be divided into three stages. Although how each bitch undergoes each stage may differ, each stage will be recognizable to an informed observer. Labor begins with shivering, trembling, and panting. The bitch, obviously unsettled, may have a faraway, withdrawn look about her. She often seeks a dark, secluded place and begins ''nesting''—scratching and tearing at newspaper, bedding, or any available material and attempting to gather it into a nest.

Once the first stage of labor has begun, it is best to confine the mother to the room where the whelping box has been placed. If allowed the run of the house, the mother may seek, and will probably find, a spot which suits her better than the whelping box, such as under the bed, behind the couch, or in the closet and will make a nest. This behavior is a natural response to uterine cramps and even a normally well-mannered dog cannot be trusted at this time.

During the first stage of labor, the mother may want to go outside. This is normal and it will ease delivery if she defecates. However, it is essential that she be accompanied, as she may have confused the uterine cramps with the urge to defecate, and a puppy might be delivered outside. This is more apt to occur with a new mother.

The first stage of labor may continue for quite some time before the final stages of labor begin. While some bitches will carry on for ten or more hours

195

Schipperke puppies are among the most appealing of all breeds and are often described as looking like a "bear cub."

before getting down to business, others will have a puppy within the first two hours. When labor begins, the mother should be shielded from all unnecessary confusion or excitement. Strangers in the house or the presence of other dogs are upsetting to a whelping bitch and may be detrimental at this time.

The second stage, true labor, is characterized by purposeful straining. The cervix gradually opens and allows the first puppy to enter the birth canal. The vulva, which is ordinarily small and firm, has stretched and relaxed with the approach of labor so the puppies can pass without tearing the mother's tissues.

The manner in which the dog accepts labor is highly individual. Some bitches show signs of typical cramps. They may cry out or grunt and strain with concentrated effort. An occasional individual becomes hysterical. At the other extreme, "easy whelpers" may show no sign of abdominal contractions and complete labor calmly, quietly, and with little or no apparent effort. Some mothers have delivered so effortlessly that the owner was unaware of the birth until the pup cried!

During labor the bitch may lie on her side in the typical position or may squat or stand. The squatting position is more often seen with Schipperkes. Under normal conditions, after a few minutes of purposeful straining, the amniotic sac protrudes. This is followed by a few forceful, expulsive efforts which produce the pup and the placental membranes. Occasionally, however, the amniotic sac may appear, then recede into the vagina as the mother rests between contractions. This is normal. However, if there is a blackish-green discharge before any puppies are delivered, call the veterinarian immediately. This discharge is the afterbirth and may indicate a puppy is free from the placenta and must be delivered within a maximum of two hours. After the first pup is born, this discharge is normal.

When hard labor begins and the contractions become strong and regular, stand by with a towel, ready to lift the puppy away as it emerges from the vulva. If it is an easy birth, and the cord is still attached, the placenta may be eased out immediately after the puppy is born. The membrane sac over the puppy's head should be quickly broken so that the pup can breathe. The cord should be cut with sterilized scissors about two inches from the body, the mouth opened gently, and the puppy dried briskly with a towel. As soon as the puppy is breathing easily, it should be returned to the bitch so she will realize the newborn is her responsibility.

Most puppies are born head-first, but breech delivery in a dog is also normal. If the puppy is protruding tail-first, and delivery is unusually slow, it is best to help free the pup's head. Because the head is the largest part of the puppy, the rest of the body may be delivered more easily, and the mother may need to rest before delivering the head on a breech birth. Therefore, *there is some danger of a partially delivered puppy suffocating if the head is not freed quickly*. A piece of toweling should be wrapped around the visible portion of the puppy. The puppy should then be removed with a firm but gentle pull, timed to coincide with each contraction. The puppy should be pulled in an upward direction if it is on its back and in a downward direction if it is on its stomach.

Puppies who have had a difficult birth may be extremely difficult to revive. Their tongue, gums, and even the pads of their feet may have turned blue. Even though a puppy may appear to be dead, do not give up on it too quickly. Sometimes a puppy will come around after fifteen to twenty minutes of seemingly futile attempts to revive it. The puppy should be taken to another room so the mother will not be upset by what is being done.

First, the puppy should be vigorously rubbed against the hair up the back and neck with a towel. If this does not elicit a response, the puppy's air passages may be obstructed by fluids. The puppy is held firmly on its back in a towel, head down, and gently swung toward the floor several times. Any mucous and fluid expelled from the nose should be wiped away. Some breeders alternate swinging the puppy with sessions of mouth to mouth resuscitation. This is accomplished by breathing into the puppy's mouth, then pressing gently on the ribs to force the air back out. The procedure is rhythmically repeated for a minute or two before swinging the puppy again.

If the puppy starts to gasp for air, it should be massaged with a towel. Rubbing a puppy against the hair up the back of the neck will provoke the pup into crying. After the pup is breathing on its own, it can be returned to the mother. Even if the birth was normal, some Schipperke puppies are slow to start breathing. Because of this, some breeders, reluctant to tempt fate, will take the puppy away from the bitch as soon as it is born. The puppy is then returned to the dam after it has been dried off and is breathing easily on its own.

After the actual whelping process has started, some breeders place a heating pad or hot water bottle wrapped with a towel in a small cardboard box and cover the carton with a blanket. The heated box is placed by the whelping box so the first-born puppies can be kept warm and out of the bitch's way while she delivers the remainder of her litter. The bitch can be shown where her puppies are, and if she becomes agitated when a puppy in the box squeals, it can easily be put back with her. It is very important that the mother feel secure, protected, and private. "A chilled puppy is a dead puppy," is a wise adage, so remember to check the heat source periodically.

The third stage of labor immediately follows the second and is characterized by uterine rest. The mother will clean the newborn puppy, and if enough time elapses before the next delivery begins, she will allow it to nurse.

The time interval between the delivery of each puppy varies from fifteen or twenty minutes to several hours. If the bitch is resting for most of the time, all is well, but two hours of intermittent, unproductive contractions is a different matter entirely. Hard, prolonged labor will wear a bitch down quickly. If labor is allowed to go beyond three hours, the bitch may be having a difficult time and surgical intervention is required.

If a bitch is left to struggle through a rough delivery for a number of puppies, the odds will be that much less in favor of her surviving the surgery. Expect to pay good money for the considerable time the veterinarian will give to the whelping bitch. It is well worth it, though, to know if the bitch does not respond to the usual whelping aids given by a veterinarian, such as intravenous calcium or pitocin injections, that surgery can be performed.

Opinion is divided about letting a bitch eat the afterbirths. Some bitches will vomit or have diarrhea if allowed to eat the afterbirths, so some breeders quickly remove each afterbirth when it is passed before the bitch can get to it. Others contend that the afterbirths contain nutrients which are beneficial to the bitch after whelping. There appears to be no "right" answer, and it remains a matter of each breeder's preference.

When all the puppies have been delivered, any retained afterbirth or membranes are normally discharged by the uterus. Sometimes this function is accompanied by uterine contractions which correspond to labor. It is difficult to determine when a bitch has finished delivering a litter. The swollen horns of the uterus can feel hard and lumpy, and consequently are mistaken for being another puppy. One simple indicator is that a bitch will usually relax and quietly settle down to nurse her new family once the last puppy has been delivered. When delivery is complete, the mother should be exercised outside so that she may eliminate.

The new mother should be allowed to have absolute privacy and quiet after she has settled in with her family. This is often difficult when there are young, curious children in the family. If the bitch shows no uneasiness about children coming into the room where her puppies are, no harm will be done by letting them *quietly look* at the puppies. However, be cautious about permitting outsiders to see the puppies, gauging your restrictions to the bitch's reactions.

After labor has ceased, a professional examination is advisable to determine if any puppies or afterbirth have been retained. The puppies should also be checked by a veterinarian within twenty-four hours after birth.

POST-DELIVERY CARE

The days following whelping are a period of stress; milk production and care of her puppies present a physical and emotional strain to the mother. Proper care will ensure good health for the puppies and their mother.

The mother should spend much of her time quietly watching over her puppies, lying calmly while the puppies nurse, licking them afterwards, and allowing them to sleep undisturbed until they awaken for the next feeding. She will leave the whelping box only to relieve herself. Sometimes, she may dig and scratch in the nest (as during labor) several days after whelping. Allow the mother to choose her own level of activity. It is normal for the bitch to stay with her pups for the majority of the time for the first two or three weeks. When the puppies are about three weeks old, she will leave them for increasingly longer periods of time as part of the natural weaning process.

Occasionally, however, a mother cannot or will not provide normal maternal care. Such a dog often is restless or nervous and will continually disturb the pups. Unwilling to lie down and allow them to nurse, she may carry them around or lick them relentlessly. The abnormally nervous mother is violent and excessive in her actions and may continue them for days afterward. In her frenzy she may cause bodily harm to the puppies. If the mother is not exhibiting normal maternal care toward her pups, notify the veterinarian. Newborn life is fragile; to wait and see if the mother will calm down may spell death for the puppies.

The entire mammary area should be washed daily with a mild soap or shampoo and rinsed to be kept clean. Proper sanitation helps keep the breasts disease-free. Unclean breasts may result in mastitis, affecting the mother or puppies, resulting in diarrhea or septicemia. Daily inspection allows for early detection of mastitis before the infection can spread to the puppies via the mother's milk. Be alert for areas that are becoming hot and swollen and tender to the touch. Abnormal swelling, redness, sores, or tenderness should be brought to the attention of the attending veterinarian. Puppies should not be allowed to nurse a suspect breast until the veterinarian has examined it. Minor skin abrasions and scratches from puppy teeth or nails may lead to infection and should be treated with a skin antiseptic. The largest mammary gland is not always the best producer of milk, as milk production can only be judged by the attitude and health of the puppies. Unnursed breasts fill with milk and are firm. If not nursed, milk production ceases and reabsorption begins until the breast returns to normal size. After the puppies are weaned, the mammary glands will gradually return to normal size and shape.

Following delivery, the bitch will have some vaginal discharge. The color is normally dark green. Within twenty-four hours the discharge turns brown and appears "stringy" with mucous; some streaks of blood may be present. The discharge gradually becomes transparent and diminishes in frequency and volume. Most bitches will keep themselves clean but some may require human assistance. A daily washing may be necessary to keep the vaginal area clean and odor-free. Should the discharge be prolonged (over four weeks) or contain blood clots or pus, notify the veterinarian at once.

The mother's hair coat may become dull, and shedding may be evident about sixty days following whelping. No way has yet been found to prevent this condition. However, it is temporary, and the coat will soon return to normal. Following delivery, especially if dullness and shedding do occur, it will probably be necessary to groom the bitch more frequently.

The mother should be continued on the same diet as was fed prior to whelping, although vitamins and mineral supplements may be added to the diet at the discretion of your veterinarian. Hematinics can usually be discontinued.

As a general rule, feed the mother three times a day and offer her as much as she will eat in about ten to twenty minutes. Her liquid consumption will be increased because of milk production. Allow her free choice of fresh water at all times.

Milk in the diet is *not* required for lactation, and unusually high milk consumption can have serious adverse effects. The mother will continue her normal elimination pattern except that the increased food intake will result in more frequent bowel movements. Diarrhea in a nursing dog can cause the milk to "dry up." Therefore, it is important that the stools be watched to detect any early signs of a problem. Notify the veterinarian immediately if any trouble signs occur.

Vomiting can also "dry up" milk production through dehydration. If a nursing mother vomits more than once, notify the veterinarian.

CARE OF THE NEWBORN

Nursing puppies should be supervised to assure that all are feeding. Newborn puppies are content to sleep between feedings, and they nurse at about two-hour intervals. Nursing may be encouraged by placing the puppy on the breast. The first milk in the mother's breast is called colostrum and contains antibodies. If the puppy does not nurse from the mother initially, the puppy will miss this important maternal immunity.

There are occasions when the mother will not or cannot nurse, and bottle feeding must be used. As a rough guide, puppies should receive some nourishment in the first six hours. If they do not, and if the puppies start prolonged crying, or begin to lose muscle tone and become weak, they should be hand fed. If possible, consult the veterinarian and discuss the problem.

A number of good substitutes for bitch's milk are on the market today, and a supply of this should always be on hand prior to delivery. An emergency formula can easily be made by mixing equal volumes of warm water and evaporated milk. The formula may be fed from a baby bottle equipped with a used baby nipple or premature baby nipple. While the puppy lies prone, the bottle may be held at a slight angle, allowing the puppy to push with the front legs. Feeding should be repeated at approximately two-hour intervals.

The environmental temperature has a great influence on the puppies. A room temperature of seventy degrees or above, coupled with a conscientious bitch, will protect the puppies from chilling. If the mother leaves her puppies or if the puppies are removed from the mother for any length of time, it is important that artificial heat of approximately eighty-five degrees be furnished. The ideal method is an incubator; however, such a method is hardly practical for the individual owner. Therefore, three alternate methods that may be used, in order of preference, are: (1) heating pad, (2) infrared lamp, (3) hot-water bottle. The use of an electric heating pad is a practical method of providing auxiliary warmth and should be covered with toweling and/or a flannel jacket. This provides the puppies with a sense of security—they feel a soft and "furry" correlate to the natural body heat of the mother. Before using a heating pad, the temperature *must* be checked. Because heating pads are manufactured without a precise temperature-control device, it is possible that the pad's lowest setting could produce a temperature that could be dangerous or even fatal to newborn puppies. Puppies can become overheated and even die if they wiggle between the cover and the heating pad or get under the pad and can't get out, so it is essential to check the puppies frequently.

Another good source of heat is an infrared lamp. At a distance of about

Schipperke puppy at eight weeks of age. The ratio of height to length is as it will be in the future. The sprinkling of grown-up hairs along the spine indicates the future coat. A light eye may not appear until later, but the shape is there.

thirty inches, the lamps usually reach and sustain a temperature of about eighty-five degrees after fifteen minutes. However, these units can differ. If this method is used, carefully monitor the temperature. The lamp maintains the heat best if placed directly above the pups. While the penetrating heat of the lamp can be soothing, it has certain disadvantages. Used over a period of days, it tends to dry the puppies' skin so that emollients may be needed. Because it is radiant, the temperature is higher in the center and wanes toward the perimeter. Infrared rays can cause dangerous burns if they are too close. Hot-water bottles are a good temporary source of heat, but they are inefficient and unreliable for a long period of time.

Most puppies spend the first twenty-four hours of their life nursing or sleeping. Random movements (twitches) of the body and face are normal. The mother will stimulate elimination and respiration by licking the puppy's genitals. Pain response is slow. When their heads are stroked, puppies will squirm forward

Two puppies at eight weeks of age. Ears are usually upright at this age although some puppies' ears may not be completely upright until the end of the teething period.

(rooting reflex). Prolonged crying should be investigated. This is a distress signal and indicates discomfort such as hunger, chilling, or pain.

TAIL DOCKING

Although the Schipperke is considered as a tailless breed, most puppies are born with tails. The following description written by John H. Hensley, D.V.M., appeared in the book *The Schipperke Anthology* and is *intended* to aid a *veterinarian*. It should *never* be attempted by a novice, as it may result in permanent injury or death to the puppy.

"The Schipperke is supposed to be tailless so it should be de-tailed rather than docked as in short-tailed breeds. This technique must be performed by a competent veterinarian. De-tailing and removal of dewclaws are performed at the same time. We prefer to do these procedures at forty-eight to seventy-two hours of age as there is no shock evidenced and discomfort lasts only a minute or two and healing takes place in a minimum of time.

Materials are as follows:

1) hair clipper with size #40 blade;
2) one pair straight mosquito forceps;
3) one pair curved mosquito forceps;
4) one pair surgical scissors;
5) Needle holder and small bayonet pointed curved or half curved surgical needle and thirty six gauge stainless steel suture.

Procedure:

1) Clip hair at base of tail and small area of rump;
2) If there is any soiling present, scrub with Phisohex detergent. This is generally not necessary;
3) Extend tail parallel to body. With straight mosquito forceps from base of tail dorsally at a 45 degree angle across ventral surface, close and lock. Twist off protruding tail. Remove forceps after thirty seconds;

This bitch is four months old. The adult coat is coming in and ears are fully upright.

Puppy at five months of age.

4) With curved mosquito forceps partially open, gently force skin back to expose stump of tail. With pointed surgical scissors cut off coccyx level with rump;

5) Insert needle in medial line of ventral tail flap—draw up to cover stump—suture to midline of dorsal incision—tie firmly with surgeon's knot, and clip sutures at knot. The suture will slough with healing scab; and

6) With curved mosquito forceps crush dewclaws at base and touch with ferric subsulfate and seal.

With this simple technique we avoid embarrassment of perineum with resulting anal distortion; the active vestigial tail under the skin which constantly milks the anal glands and the bunny tailed vestige which distorts the desired ɔbby profile.''

Another method used by some breeders is the banding method. It should *not* be attempted without the aid of a veterinarian or a breeder who is thoroughly experienced in the method.

WEANING THE LITTER

At three weeks, the pups may be offered some food. The larger the litter, the sooner they may want to eat, although most are ready by four weeks. There are special puppy preparations on the market, but alternatives such as high protein baby cereal, or warm and properly diluted evaporated milk flavored with a little strained baby liver, may be fed. The first meal is usually an unsuccessful mess, so don't mix much. The puppies may actually acquire their first real taste of food by licking it off each other.

Offer food once or twice a day until it becomes obvious that they want it. All pups should be eating well by five weeks but do not force the bitch to wean them. She will do so gradually, usually completing the process by the sixth week.

A bitch may test worm free, but many puppies have Roundworms. Puppies should be wormed at five weeks. The veterinarian can prescribe the proper medication and dosage.

Puppies should be socialized with people and other animals. These two puppies are making each other's acquaintance.

EVALUATION

The pups may now be ready for their new homes at eight weeks. Quality can be better judged at this age than it can again for some time. The ears in most puppies are up at this time. The baby teeth usually can indicate whether or not there is a proper bite. The ratio of height to length is as it will be in the future. After two months of age, the puppy enters the gawky, "teen-age" growth stage, when everything seems out of proportion. The sprinkling of grown-up hairs along the spine indicates the future coat. A light eye may not appear until much later, but the shape is there.

Watch the gait as the puppy moves. How does the pup stop and pose when a strange noise is heard? A future champion often stands out in the litter. A standout is *not* necessarily the most perfect—no one is: A standout has that elusive, indefinable, all-important, joyous quality of showmanship; that's the one to keep!